Figure It Out

Seven Key Factors That Fashioned My Life

Figure It Out

Seven Key Factors That
Fashioned My Life

*My Journey From The Trailer Park To
Becoming A Woman Of Influence*

Trista Sue Kragh

Maverick Press 2015

Cover and Graphics Design by: Matthew H Kragh
Author's Photo by: Rochelle Shucart Photography

Maverick Press 2015

ISBN: 978-0-9965392-0-3

Printed in the United States of America
First Edition Printing: July, 2015

CONTENTS

DEDICATION 7

ACKNOWLEDGMENTS 9

INTRODUCTION 11

Chapter 1 - MY STORY 15

Chapter 2 - PRINCIPLE OF PRINCIPLES 25

Chapter 3 - FIGURE IT OUT 37

Chapter 4 - PAY ATTENTION 59

Chapter 5 - TELL IT LIKE IT IS 75

Chapter 6 - SHOW ME YOUR FRUIT 97

Chapter 7 - DREAM BIG, BUILD SMALL 117

Chapter 8 - SAFEST PLACE ON EARTH 135

Chapter 9 - WHO IS YOUR SOURCE? 151

CONCLUSION 165

APPENDIX 167

The Kingdom of God Ambassador's Pledge 167

Recommended Readings 169

About The Author 170

Resources From Trista Sue 171

Figure It Out

DEDICATION

To a true Proverbs 31 woman who set the standard high: *The late Jill C. Youngquist,* my mom, who kept me grounded in God's WORD as she lived and breathed it.

I am a product of the love and support of these four amazing men in my life that showed they believed in me:

- *Tim G. Youngquist,* my dad: You gave me life and trained me to think and act for myself. It is because of this training in certain key mentalities that I will continually strive to become all I was born to be.

- *Matthew Kragh,* my amazing husband: Thank you for giving me the freedom to be who I am, and for being extremely supportive of the vision.

- *Maverick Kragh,* my precious gift and beloved son, whom I empower daily to *'figure it out'.*

- *The late Dr. Myles Munroe,* my mentor and spiritual father, whom I lovingly refer to as *"Papa Myles"*: He embodied what he taught and allowed me to observe and travel with him as he taught the original truth. This book would simply not exist without him commissioning me.

ACKNOWLEDGMENTS

I am honored to acknowledge the following special people in my vision:

Each leader at *Kingdom Community International* in Naples, Florida and various nations: You are diligent *mentees* who make the vision possible and the journey worthwhile. Each one is a true agent of change and that makes me so proud. I am truly honored to serve you. "I can see further than my eyes can look."

Finally, I would not be able to accomplish the vision for my life if it was not for the sacrifice and dedication of *Debra Kay Horner*, who walked by my side at the most transitional time in my life. You are truly one sent by God whom I cherish.

And last but not least: *Everyone who is bored with life and wondering whether there is more to it than this.* There is.... Here is my journey with seven key life lessons and principles that fashioned it.

INTRODUCTION

I have never had the desire to write a book, although I knew it was something that had to be done. It seems like everyone, young and old, is writing a book. Well, if everyone is doing it, then I am one who has no desire to join in. I enjoy doing things completely different from the acceptable norm. I have heard these questions and comments repeatedly over the past ten years:

"So when are you going to write a book?"

"You need to write a book."

I would simply smile and say, "Yes, I know. Others have said the same thing." I do not know whether this is a common thing to be told, but in the back of my mind I knew I would write a book at some point, but only when I had something worth putting on the pages.

Well, the time finally came on August 7, 2014 while I was in the Bahamas. I had just finished my session as a guest speaker at a conference hosted by my mentor, the Late Dr. Myles Munroe. He summoned me to his hospitality room and said:

"Trista, you have to write a book!"

My heart sank; alas, the time had come. He continued,

"I know the title."

My heart leaped! How did he know that was the missing ingredient in the back of my mind? I had been wondering what aspect of my life or which topics I would write about. Dr. Munroe continued,

"You should title it *Figure It Out* and just share the lessons that you have learned in life."

In my mind I thought - 'Oh! That's easy; I have a ton of stories.' I had just shared with the audience how as a youth, my father's response to the majority of the problems I presented to him was to simply "figure it out," and I have certainly spent most of my life "figuring it out."

My mind struggled with the thought of going through the process of actually writing the book. So I mumbled to Dr. Munroe under my breath,

"I do not want to write a book. Do I have to write a book?"

I am quite vocal with my thoughts. I knew I probably shouldn't share these with him; however, I could not help myself. He responded:

"I used to say the same thing. However, if you do not write it, I will. You have six months to get it done."

OH NO! Not only has he told me what I must do, but he's given me a time limit too? Okay, I guess I will have to *figure it out!*

In this book, I provide practical solutions and guidance that will hopefully enable you to move away from the rat race of life, and find pure joy by discovering your life assignment, so you can truly manifest your full potential before you leave this earth. You will find seven life lessons that I believe can help you move from the point of making a living to truly start living. If you are able to figure it out then you will make this book worth being written.

A considerable amount of the principles I share are from the teachings and words of wisdom that I received from my spiritual father and mentor, the Late Dr. Myles Munroe. I am a product of his teachings, as well as the number of lessons learned from my biological father and mother.

Although this book is about me, it is written for you! I would love to hear from you. My contact information is listed in the appendix.

- *Trista Sue*

Chapter 1

MY STORY

"You've always had the power my dear; you just had to learn it for yourself."
- Glinda, Wizard of Oz

My parents were twenty-one years old when I was born. They were young, in love and working diligently to make ends meet. During this time my father was drilling shallow, residential water wells with a small stomper rig. He used his income to design and build his first rotary well rig in the back yard of our little wooden home. His mom signed a $10,000 note to help get the hydraulics built on the rig. This is how my father's water-well drilling company got started. As it grew, he never splurged to buy luxury items. He would put whatever income he received back into the business to purchase more equipment.

I recall being in the ninth grade when my father came home one night and announced that he had won the bid for a *deep-injection well* for the city of St. Petersburg, Florida. This involves the process of disposing wastewater deep underground. It meant he would become the deepest injection driller of 1,100 ft. Today he is preparing to drill 10,000 ft.

That night my father announced he would become the 'Sewer King.'

I then asked if that would make me a 'Sewer Princess.'

He said, "Yes, of course."

I then asked, "Does a sewer princess get a ring?"

He said, "Absolutely."

Sure enough I received an emerald ring as my first piece of jewelry, and I became a 'Sewer Princess.' I still have that precious ring as a keepsake.

My early childhood began in a little wooden house that my grandparents owned. One morning when my mom retrieved me from my crib she discovered my bottles had holes in them from the rats chewing them. After that incident I slept in their bathroom. When I was a toddler, we moved into my grandmother's mobile home park known as 'Harvey Heights.' This was a big step up in our world as we moved into a double-wide trailer, whereas all the other trailers were single-wide.

I had a wonderful childhood playing with my sister in Harvey Heights. We rode our bikes, had a tree with a swing and a pool to play with our cousins in the hot summers. As I became old enough to attend school, my father did not want me to attend the same public school that he once attended. So my mom found a new little Christian private school and enrolled me in kindergarten. That was the beginning of my relationship with God our Father. That year I gave my life to the Lord in my little kindergarten class where I became the first Christian in my family. I remember to this day saying the prayer and committing my life to Jesus. By the end of that school year we could recite the entire Psalms 23, The Lord is my shepherd, by memory. I also remember always talking and singing to God throughout my childhood. My heart has always remained tender to Him.

My father is a very extreme man and an independent thinker who thrives on challenges. He's always thinking ahead and outside the box. When he gave instructions to my younger sister and me, we jumped immediately and completed the task. We learned to never ask him 'how' or 'why' or 'when'. It was all about completing the task immediately; we had to just *figure it out* for ourselves. I therefore grew up with the mindset that I could accomplish anything that was asked of me. After all, my father was not in the habit of showing us how to do everything. Therefore, the capability is inherently set in; all I had to do is utilize my brain. It never mattered how young I was or even that I was a girl. My father did not treat me different because of my gender. He expected the same results and capabilities as if I were a boy. These were never a factor in his mind.

Reflecting back today, I realize this is why I have no limitations or excuses for anything. These factors never existed in my childhood. By age nine, I was driving my dad's little yellow Isuzu manual (stick shift) car on the back roads of our neighborhood all by myself. He taught me how to shift the gears in driving, and then I practiced to perfect it, although I did slightly bump another parked car once.

Every summer I worked at my father's machine shop where they fabricate most of the equipment for his water well drilling company. At age twelve, I was milling metal squares on the lathe machines and cutting my fingers on the extremely sharp metal shavings. However, crying never worked with my father. Tough love was the only way he knew how to operate.

As a teenager, I was driving heavy equipment to level our 700-acre dirt-fill pit on a motor grader. Oh boy, were those some long hours in the heat of South Florida's summer sun. I worked every weekday from 7 am until 5 pm. My sister and I would never dream of clocking in at 7:01 am; we knew we would be in big trouble! Unfortunately, whenever I did something that I should not have, I would always get caught. This, I believe, is the result of a praying mother. So I finally figured if I did not want to get in trouble, then I should not do bad things.

My father did not have an ounce of patience. Sometimes my sister and I were left in a restaurant if we had not finished eating at the same time as my dad, so he would just leave us there as he got in his car and headed back to work. Eating a meal got in the way when it came to my father's work; it slowed him down. I remember being at the Burger King drive through window one day and I could not decide on my order fast enough, so we did not get to eat.

My father is a risk taking, no-nonsense, extremely frugal, tell-it-like-it-is man whose emotions are just not his strong suit. His attire has not changed much over the years. He has been wearing blue jeans, sneakers, and a baseball cap since his youth. My dad never had a desk or his own office. He's very private with his personal life and keeps his thoughts to himself. Dad is like a human vault. You never know what he's thinking or what business or project he is developing next. It is guaranteed that he is working on something big and sometimes random.

On the other hand, my mother was the complete opposite of my father. She was petite, innocent, extremely shy, very beautiful, and soft-spoken. I recall when she became radically saved when I was close to age nine; it happened a few years after me. She then started taking my sister and me to the local McGregor Baptist Church. Mom was very focused on understanding the Word of God to keep her marriage and family together. She faithfully attended the weekly Bible studies and would always invite some of the ladies over to our house, showing them what she had learned from the Word. From there, most of the ladies in our families came to know Jesus. She went from watching soap operas to having conversations and praying for others on the phone. I learned a lot about God just by overhearing her conversations. Mom always had praise and worship music on in the house, that is, until dad came home from work. She kept the atmosphere in our home peaceful. My sister and I were forbidden to watch MTV or listen to secular music. I remember when we moved out of the trailer park and into a beautiful new home when I was in the seventh grade. One day mom had invited numerous African-American women over and she was baptizing them in our new pool. That day my father stopped by during lunchtime and as he entered the door and saw everyone in the pool, he walked back out the door. He probably did not know what to think of all the commotion.

BE FEARLESS

My father instilled a spirit of fearlessness within my sister and me. I was water skiing and had my own motorcycle by age five. Once we were water skiing in a lake that had alligators, which are common in our region. When I told Dad I did not want to ski in the lake, he replied, "Get in the water, you will be fine." I believed him. So I did, and I guess you can see I was fine.

My childhood is filled with numerous stories like this and every time my dad was right. He never allowed us to operate with fear or let it dictate our actions. Therefore, taking risks becomes natural to me. I have lived a full life, traveled the world and done some crazy things. I have done shark free-diving in the Bahamas, parachuted tandem off of a mountain in New-Zealand, jumped off bridges and cliffs, raced boats, cars, and drove any vehicle as fast I could once my hands were behind the wheel. However, life-threatening situations are different in that we should always use wisdom and never put ourselves in harms way.

My family's extreme thinking was normal for me, and it still is to some degree. I am focused and results orientated. I do not allow anything or anyone to slow me down or get in the way of my goal. So in that sense people may consider me perhaps a bit hardheaded and tenacious. But I prefer to classify it as being narrow minded. I have found this to be a prerequisite in life when it comes to my life vision.

I graduated from the little Christian school at age eighteen with no plans for attending college, because I was in love. Somehow, my father could read the writing on the wall, so he instructed my mother to send me anywhere I wanted to go as long as it was outside the state of Florida. One day I came home and heard Richard Roberts on television talking about the Oral Roberts University enrollment for the upcoming coming semester. My mom said, "Trista, how about ORU?" I immediately started crying, for in this moment, I knew that was the right choice, although I would have to leave the boyfriend who was my world.

Two weeks later I was on a plane, with a broken hand (from a competitive racquetball game with a friend's father) leaving home for the first time to stay in a foreign place with only one acquaintance I knew from my church. Lori and I became friends during this journey as we became roommates. When I arrived in Tulsa, Oklahoma, I still was not completely accepted at ORU, because I had not taken my SAT exam since attending college was not a part of my future plans. Once on the campus, the school arranged for me to take the test. I had not prepared for the test, yet I knew I was supposed to be at ORU and would somehow get a decent score. My premonition was correct. I attended the school for four years, and I met some of the most amazing people from around the world. And, I eventually broke up with the boy from home who ended up cheating on me.

The lesson learned: **Never let anyone get in the way of your destiny.** I would be in a completely different place in my life today if I had not been obedient to my authority (my dad) and the Holy Spirit. (I will address this later).

I graduated from Oral Roberts University in 1995, armed with a Health and Exercise Degree, and I had no idea what I was going to do with my life. I returned home not knowing the next aspect of my life journey. So I spent the summer with my mom and we went to church, and I attended numerous prayer meetings that she led and Bible studies.

My father had left my mom during my senior year of high school, and when he heard that I was not doing much for the summer, he sent me out to the grapefruit and orange grove that he owned. I spent that summer working in a little 10' x 20' job site trailer from 7 a.m. until 5 p.m. every day. I tested the chemistry of the fruit juiced by measuring the size of the grapefruit from different areas of the grove to analyze when and where we could start picking the fruit to sell to the packers.

There I was at age 21 working amongst the snakes and alligators in a grapefruit grove with a college degree and no clue of my purpose. At one point we had so much rain, it was over saturating the ground in all of Florida's fruit groves. This was a huge problem in that the fruit would not be good enough for harvest and we could lose the entire crop, which was 1 mile by 1 mile in size. I decided that I could use my influence with my Heavenly Father to pray for the rain to stop at our grove. Can you guess what happened? That week a fruit packer company representative came to our office looking for fruit to purchase. He pointed at the weather radar screen and declared we were the only spot in South Florida that did not get the down pours that week. Our property was located on the corner of the county line, so it was very easy to spot our grove from the radar. He then mentioned that someone must be praying. My dad just looked at me and I smiled. I did not have to say anything.

My father had co-ownership with a few partners of a hotel in Naples, so in October that year he suggested that I tour the property. I had heard about it, but I could not recall visiting it until then. So my mom and I made a thirty-five mile trip South to check out this 101 room Comfort Inn hotel painted the color of a pink Pepto-Bismol bottle. It was hideous! I worked at the Front Desk during an interim when the management company was being terminated by the partners. My task was to make sure things went smoothly during this transition. In my mind, I planned on being there for three weeks and then start working somewhere in a ministry.

Guess what happened? Twenty years later and I am still there! The partners hired a new general manager, with whom I worked as his assistant in his office for seven months. We terminated an incompetent head housekeeper who subsequently sued us for sexual harassment. The new general manager resigned upon the news. I called my father and told him we needed to find a new general manager. Dad's response was, "Trista, stand up and do the job. Figure it out." And that was it as the conversation ended.

I was twenty-two years old, and the last thing I wanted was the responsibility of managing a hotel. We had just completed an addition of a bar with a water-view terrace. I have never had a drink in my life, what do I know about running a bar? It did not matter. Saying 'no' to my dad was not an option. There I was very young with only seven months experience becoming the general manager of a destination hotel in downtown Naples, Florida.

What a journey this has been. I have been lied to, stolen from, yelled at by guests for being a woman manager, called names, taken advantage of, the mayor and locals were mad at me for someone had slandered me, which reached the media and was featured in our newspapers and local nightly news.

Sometimes guests can be very confrontational and even lie just to get a free night. Once someone brought a white rat into their room just to say it was found there so they could get a free night. Another man insisted an iguana crawled into his room during the night and was on top of him. Later, he called me to apologize. He must have seen a lizard that day and had a bad dream that he thought was real. Oh, the list goes on and on and on. I am sure I have forgotten more than I can remember.

Numerous renovations have been done, which involves dealing with contractors, liars, swindlers and incompetence. I have had to figure out everything from electrical issues, plumbing, hot water heaters exploding, safety issues, you name it. We could have done a very successful reality TV series over the past twenty years. Anyone who thinks running a hotel is glamorous is in for a big surprise; they have no idea the responsibility and stress one must endure.

You might be surprised to know that within the first several years I turned in my resignation to the partners three separate times. I was restless in my spirit, because I could not see how managing a hotel validated me as doing God's work. Each time I resigned, God shut the doors on me. He honored my prayers for His will to be done, rather than my will. My dilemma was trying to imagine facing God on judgment day when He would ask what I did with my life. In my mind, my response was, "Put heads in bed." That was not a suitable answer for me, so I fought it. Then something happened. My father bought the four partners interest in the hotel, which allowed me the freedom and liberty to do whatever I wanted. I could renovate, give discounts to pastors and missionaries. Awesome!

> "If you are what you should be, you will set the whole world on fire."
> - St Catherine of Siena

My father's philosophy for the most part when he told me to run the hotel was '*laissez-faire.*' This is French for "Let us be, let us do," or "hands-off" in my translation. He trusted that I would do the very best of my ability and use my best judgment. He was not constantly over my shoulder watching or questioning everything I did. He trained me, thus he could trust me. I have made many mistakes at the hotel; all were part of the learning experience. The hotel has not burned down and it has never gone bankrupt. I always call my dad once a year to let him know how much profit we earned, and I ask his permission to do major renovations.

I eventually discovered that the hotel was my ministry to the employees, our guests, and the international community. I have learned to use this resource I have been given stewardship of for the Kingdom of God. Now, it's game on! I am doing the best of my ability to add value to what I have been given responsibility over.

I am so thankful that I never left the business world. It has been an invaluable amount of experience, and I now understand how it has prepared me for my life assignment. Working at a church would have never prepared me for what God has purposed for me to accomplish for Him.

In the off-season summer months, I was extremely bored; my travels expanded all over the world, and I sometimes found myself in some unfortunate situations. Reflecting back, I now see that my purpose was definitely not known during my 20's age bracket. I was extremely bored and found time for a lot of drama. My life was like a soap opera. I matured a bit in my thirties, got married and discovered my purpose when I discovered myself through Dr. Myles Munroe's mentorship. Now in my forties, my life is more fulfilling and very exciting. I am executing my purpose and passion, and nothing is more satisfying. It feels good to know that I have been able to find my way simply by adhering to God's principles of life.

Chapter 2

PRINCIPLE OF PRINCIPLES

*"God didn't want success in life to be haphazard but predictable. So He
built in life laws & principles. Operate life in principles, not effort."*
-Dr. Myles Munroe

You are about to embark upon my most impactful life lessons,
but first I must clarify the importance of principles in life. This is, by
far, the most important fundamental truth I have discovered, and it
has made a profound difference in my life.

Religion is easily used to complicate the simple things of God.
We grasp at scriptures here and there in an attempt to merge them
into information that will help us figure things out. I can remember
times past when I was always trying to find that missing piece of a
puzzle just to fix a situation or to make sense of a difficulty I was
facing. I had a lot of questions and I needed some answers. I wanted
to know when God would ever come through and answer my
prayers. Why does nothing seem to work out right for me? We spend
most of our life in church, yet it seems as though we are not getting
anywhere. But we can definitely be found in the pews on Sunday
morning singing, praying and tarrying.

God did not create life to be complicated or a mystery. He created everything in life to succeed. That is the reason for us having His principles to guide us in life; we are guaranteed success. They are also known as the Laws of God, keys or principles. God's Laws are built into creation.

Let's take a closer look at the word *principle*. Principle is derived from the word *prince*, which means *sovereign, ruler, first* or *original.* The Greek word is *ache* meaning *'that which covers you.'* Therefore, principles are the fundamental laws, foundation or base that makes everything work in life. They are the original foundational laws by which everything stands in God's creation.

Success in life is predictable if you know and activate the principles of life. Likewise, failure is predictable by looking at a person's bad habits. If you constantly break the laws of good health by smoking, you can predict that you will eventually get cancer.

Principles are permanent; facts change. Facts are the present state of a thing or situation, which is always subject to changing, whereas a principle will always out-live the facts. Life is so much easier and less emotional when you live by principles, because then the facts won't affect you. **If you stand on the principle of a thing, you will always be protected (covered) by the principle.**

This reminds me of the parable that Jesus told about the wise and foolish builders. Both men heard the words of life that Jesus spoke, however the only difference between them was the wise one applied them to his life. The foolish man was not successful because his life was not built on the foundational truth of applying the principles or keys that Jesus taught. His entire life fell apart when a crisis arrived.

In God's creation plan, a plant will grow properly if it is planted in the soil, and has access to water and sun. The plant does not have to do anything but abide by the laws of nature in order to become what it was designed to be.

This is the same program that God set up with mankind. It is the reason why Jesus said to focus on two things in life: "Seek the Kingdom and His righteousness"[1]. Righteousness is a legal word for 'right-standing.' I make a conscious effort to do my best in obeying the commands of God, so I can be sure to remain in right standing with Him. In the same way, if you are driving around town, you do not have to worry about abiding by the driving laws, but you are aware of them and subconsciously abiding by them. I should not be stressed about getting a ticket for speeding if I am not exceeding the speed limit. But being aware of the limits helps me to stay within that speed. I understand the meaning of a red light, how to properly pass a car or change lanes. I do not have to drive around always worried about whether I am going to break a driving law. I know what they are and they have become a way of learned driving behavior.

Just as we have to abide by driving laws, so do we have to abide by God's Laws. You know that forgiveness does not exclude your spouse, your siblings, in-laws, your boss or best friend. You must forgive others unconditionally at all times. You must love the Lord your God with all your heart and never do anything to contradict this. You must abide by the Golden Rule. This is a conscious decision I have to make when I am wronged or when someone has taken advantage of me. I have had to work through these things at various times in life and make sure my heart is right with others and God. The tough part is when your flesh wants to get revenge, gossip and retaliate.

God has given every human a conscious that knows innately what is wrong and right. This is an awareness of your actions and behaviors. People may choose to ignore it, but it is there. If I respond wrongly to a situation, I know instantly. It manifests in different ways; sometimes, it can be what my mom called a 'sandpaper feeling'

---

[1] Matthew 6:33

in my heart, or by feeling a heaviness. Whatever it is, my mind is constantly thinking about it. Sometimes the muscles in my shoulder will become tense and knotted. My spirit innately knows and sometimes my body responds to it.

Bitterness and un-forgiveness are two of the most destructive responses that affect you more than your offender. The Bible even notes that envy rots your bones[2]. Another translation says that jealousy is like cancer in the bones[3]. Who has time to deal with that or any other offenses?

These are some basic examples of obeying the Laws of God. The beauty of obeying them is that success is automatically built into the principles or Laws of God. Notice, I use a capital L when referring to the Laws of God. This is the difference between the traditional laws of man that religion created. I'm sure you have heard some people say, "We are not under the law". Which law is being referenced? For there are two types of laws: Divine Laws of God and ceremonial laws that religion created. We are no longer under ceremonial laws. However, we must not negate the Divine Laws of God. This is the first thing He gave Israel when they became a nation, the 10 Principles or Laws of God, Ten Commandments.

Jesus knew man would create his own gospel and abolish the Laws of God, so He addressed this in Matthew 5:17, "Do not think that I have come to abolish the Law or the Prophets; I have not come to abolish them but to fulfill them." Jesus is saying it should not even cross your mind for a millisecond that the Laws of God aren't applicable anymore. He's referring to the Divine Laws of God. Then He summed up the Laws in Matthew 22:37-40, NIV.

"Jesus replied: 'Love the Lord your God with all your heart and with all your soul and with all your mind.' This is the first and

---

[2] Proverbs 14:30
[3] Proverbs 14:30 NLT

greatest commandment. And the second is like it: 'Love your neighbor as yourself.' All the Law and the Prophets hang on these two commandments."

The capital L appears again in Law. Human nature wants to rebel and oppose authority. There is no obedience in democracy, we just cooperate with authority. Democracy is built on and encourages opposition. We then bring this same spirit into the Kingdom of God and justify our actions by quoting scriptures about 'grace'. Grace was given to obey the Law. It is not to be used as an excuse to disobey the Laws of God. The word 'grace' means *ability*. God gives you the ability to obey His Laws; the *ability* (grace) to fulfill your life assignment.

Which one of the Laws is no longer relevant? Murder, lying, adultery? When you stop obeying the Laws you destroy your country. When crimes go up, taxes increase. Breaking the Laws brings poverty to a nation. However, these same Laws make a home, community and ultimately a nation stronger and into the fulfillment of prosperity.

The church has become just as lawless as the world and we wonder why people consider us hypocrites? We wonder why we are so ineffective in being a light to our community. Unfortunately, we behave just like the world. I recently watched a documentary titled "(Dis)Honesty - the Truth About Lies" regarding research conducted over the last 5 years by The Kenan Institute for Ethics at Duke University. I was shocked to learn that their research shows that 90% of people lie, regardless of they are of religious affiliation or not. So it is the same statistic across the board! I was shocked. 90%! This should not be so.

Obeying the Laws or principles of God is for your benefit. There are consequences for disobeying the Laws of God. Judgment is built within them. Some people confuse this with God punishing them. He does not have to; they bring the consequences on themselves. We must stop blaming God and others for problems that are caused by our own bad decisions. When we know the principles of God, life works for us and we learn to make decisions based on them. Gravity is an excellent example of one of the Laws of creation. If you try to violate gravity by jumping off a 40-story building, gravity will violate you. You will be severely injured if not dead. Nobody killed you; you killed yourself by violating a law of creation. God did not punish you either. So stop looking for the devil in your problems, just look for the Laws. If you do not know which one to use, ask the Holy Spirit. He is your Helper; He will lead and guide you to all truth.

I learned a valuable lesson in 2006. My mother had been diagnosed with cancer, and she did not want to receive conventional medical treatment. Her choice was an alternative treatment found in Tijuana, Mexico. I traveled with her and was the liaison with the doctors and just stayed by her side. My sister and I, along with my brother-in-law alternated weeks being with her. We did not know the cancer stage at that time since she had not received an official medical diagnosis by a cancer facility in the USA. However, we supported her decisions and stayed by her side for one year of suffering.

This transpired during the time that I had just completed a $3M renovation at the hotel. I had dropped the franchise brand and became an independent boutique hotel. I went from operating a Comfort Inn to the Bayfront Inn Fifth Avenue. Fifth Avenue is the address and the main downtown destination for Naples. This was very important when re-branding the hotel. However, another hotel on the same street was not happy with the name I choose, so they served me with a Federal lawsuit. That hotel was the Inn On Fifth and they thought this would cause confusion by their guests when trying to book a room. They claimed I was trying to steal their customers. My intentions of just wanting the location in the hotel's new name were pure and with no other reason.

The timing of this lawsuit along with my mother's health could not have been worse, especially when having to deal with depositions. I was upset knowing the time needed to devote to my mother's care. One day, as I was blow drying my hair and meditating on the chain of events, I complained to God as I said, "God, I don't have time for this. What is the key to make this go away?" Then immediately the scripture came to my mind "pray for those who persecute you."[4] EUREKA! "That's it." I exclaimed! I instantly knew this was the key to overcoming this lawsuit. I was innocent, for I never intended to steal the other hotel's customers. I do not think like that at all! So I immediately prayed for the owner, his family and his business. Yes, I prayed for my competition. Crazy, isn't it? Yes, but I understand the principles and they always go against our reasoning. I never had to go through any depositions or through the Federal court process. The Plaintiff settled out of court for a nominal fee, and I went about my business of caring for mom.

> "The Kingdom of God defies your logic and all odds."
> -Trista Sue

When you obey the Laws of God you live under a different code. Your obedience violates all reasoning. It contradicts the status quo. Obedience is not reasonable, but it activates a law. It also reduces stress and puts the pressure on the one who gave the command. You can have confidence; you can relax and sleep well at night. While others are harboring grudges, you are forgiving. While the world stockpiles and hoards, you are giving things away. It's a different lifestyle in the Kingdom.

---

[4] Matthew 5:44b

Old Testament tells a story about Elijah and the widower who had two meals left for her and her son to eat then die[5]. Elijah did not bring her groceries; neither did he pray for her. He asked her to give him a portion of her last meal. She simply obeyed and this activated the principle of giving. Then God provided for her needs until the next rain. This violates reasoning, but it activates a law, which allowed God to intervene on her behalf.

Faith is required to live like this! We are not lacking resources on the earth, but we lack faith and obedience. If you can only see what you see, then you will hang onto what you have. The world says you should eat the last two meals. The secrets of the Kingdom say if you cannot meet your own needs, then put it in a system that multiplies back. Give it away. The pressure was on God to deliver when the widower obeyed. The ball was in His court and He was fully capable to deliver – not once but every time! But it requires having 100% trust. Child-like faith is the key. Jesus said, "Unless you change and become like little children, you will never enter the kingdom of heaven."[6] Oh I hope you grasp this imperative statement. I believe this may be a primary reason why many people get stuck in life. They try to make decisions based on reason, rather than child-like obedience. They try to negotiate with God and justify their actions. That will be a long, hard life. I learned this a long time ago, so I am always giving things away. Rather than trading in my cars, I give them to someone in need. Likewise with clothes, furniture, iPhones, etc…. give, give, give!

My main priority in life is to learn the principles of God and obey them. I cannot stress how this has simplified my life and made success inevitable. This is the right-standing part of the formula. Some people have a misconception that I live a privileged life

---

[5] I Kings 17:7-16
[6] Matthew 18:3

because of my family's success. If they only knew that **success comes by remaining in right-standing with God which means having to make the right decisions that are sometimes very difficult, following your passion and obeying principles.** That's really it in a nutshell; pure and immediate obedience. "If you love me you will obey me."[7] It is important to know that God is not a respecter of people. He has created a system to work for your benefit, so you do not have to spend your life at a miserable job toiling or scheming to get ahead. The key to your deliverance is obedience, not money. When you grasp this concept, you can live your life and fulfill your purpose. You will become concerned with making a difference, rather than trying to figure out how you are going to pay bills. Then you will see how money works for you, rather than you spending your life working for it. We were born with the dominion mandate over everything on the earth. How did we ever fall so low and get everything so backwards?

Another problem that religious people face is that they try to replace the Laws with prayer. When you know the laws you do not even have to pray for certain things. Some people will get upset when they read this, so allow me show you what Jesus said.

> "This is what the kingdom of God is like. A man scatters seed on the ground. Night and day, whether he sleeps or gets up, the seed sprouts and grows, though he does not know how. All by itself the soil produces grain—first the stalk, then the head, then the full kernel in the head. As soon as the grain is ripe, he puts the sickle to it, because the harvest has come."(Mark 4:26-29)

Man's responsibility is to simply plant the seeds. He is activating the principle of seed time and harvest. Once the seed is planted, law takes over, so he can go about his business. Jesus never said man

---

[7] John 14:15

needs to fast or pray for the seed to grow. His only responsibility is activating it.

Another example is creating life wherein the responsibility of a married couple is to conceive, to activate the law of life. Then law takes over and creates a human being while you go about your business for 9 months. How beautiful is that?

Jesus said, "The knowledge of the secrets of the kingdom of heaven has been given to you, but not to them."[8] The world is clueless of these principles of God. Many do not want to know, which is why Jesus spoke to the masses in parables. However, to those seeking the Truth of God, He will reveal the secrets of the kingdom of heaven. Here are two scriptures to support this principle of obedience.

> "The Lord said to Moses, "Speak to the Israelites and say to them: 'I am the Lord your God. You must not do as they do in Egypt, where you used to live, and you must not do as they do in the land of Canaan, where I am bringing you. Do not follow their practices. You must obey my laws and be careful to follow my decrees. I am the Lord your God. Keep my decrees and laws, for the person who obeys them will live by them."[9]

We cannot have the same lifestyle, attitude or behavior system of the world. We don't isolate ourselves from it; however we ought to be different. This is when our light is bright. We stick out from the norm because we have righteousness, peace and joy in the Holy Spirit despite our setbacks. This is the Kingdom of God.[10]

This next scripture brings peace to my soul when I read God's simple instruction to Joshua after Moses died. He was left in charge

---

[8] Matthew 13:11
[9] Leviticus 18: 1-5
[10] Romans 14:17

of millions of Israelites.

> "Be strong and very courageous. Be careful to obey all the law my servant Moses gave you; do not turn from it to the right or to the left, that you may be successful wherever you go. Keep this Book of the Law always on your lips; meditate on it day and night, so that you may be careful to do everything written in it. Then you will be prosperous and successful."[11]

God ties obedience of the laws to success. I rest my case.

I cannot emphasize the difference that understanding this fundamental truth of principles has made in my life. I live with so much more peace. When you read the parables that Jesus told, always look for the principle behind the story. Then you will have the keys to life that Jesus referred to.

I hope I have conveyed the simplicity of activating principles in your life in order to achieve the successful and abundant life that God intended for every human. The remainder of this book is a series of life lessons and principles that have made the biggest impact on my life. There are many more, but I wanted to convey those that have been paramount in my life.

---

[11] Joshua 1:7-8

PRINCIPLE RECAP

1. Success in life is predicable if you know the principles of God.

2. The secret to success is Laws.

3. Focus on two things in life - seeking the Kingdom and staying in right standing with your King.

4. There are two types of laws: Divine Laws of God and ceremonial laws that religion created.

5. Do not negate the Divine Laws of God.

6. There are consequences for disobeying the Laws of God. Judgment is built within them.

7. When you obey the Laws of God, you live under a different code.

8. Obedience is not reasonable, but it activates a Law.

9. Your main priority in life is to learn the principles of God and obey them.

10. The key to your deliverance is obedience.

11. Obedience cannot be replaced with prayer or fasting.

12. God ties obedience of the laws to success

Chapter 3

FIGURE IT OUT

Life Lesson #1

"I do not feel obliged to believe that the same God who has endowed us with sense, reason, and intellect has intended us to forgo their use."
-Galileo

The expression *'figure it out'* was familiar to my ears while growing up. It was my father's answer to a majority of the dilemmas we found ourselves in, or for any instructions he gave us. As teenagers, he always made us work every summer, either at his fabrication shop, a task at the house or at the fill-dirt pit (I refer to as the pit). For a long time I was in charge of the yard in our new house and my sister was in charge of keeping the pool clean.

When I was younger I would answer the phones at the water-well drilling company. That was fun especially since the office had air-conditioning. Another summer my dad put me in charge of 'the cage.' This was the inventory area caged-off for the sprinkler division. I set up the inventory count and a system for the workers on the sprinkler crew to be accountable for keeping their trucks stocked based on their jobs each day. The worst was when I was 16 and had the responsibility of leveling 700 acres of the pit with a motor-grader while my sister ran the air-conditioned, tinted-windowed tractor with a radio!

Oh life just wasn't fair working long, hot, arduous summer days. We hated it, especially since all of our friends were at the beach or the mall. The only thing that got me through those days was Janet Jackson's new album *Rhythm Nation*. My mom was not around and that was as rebellious as I could be, which was big for us. However, with all the various responsibilities, no matter what situations arose that left me not sure how to proceed, his response was simply, "figure it out". This became a habit during my various childhood adventures.

While in college and on spring break in 1995, I invited a group of girl friends to come home with me for the week. Dad said I could take his speedboat out. He did not come to put it in the water for me, but over my lifetime I had seen him put a boat in the water numerous times. It was a long race-boat and if I wanted to use it, I had to figure out how to back it into the water. A long boat trailer hitched to a truck can be a little tricky at times, but I did it. So the girls and I took off to Ft. Myers Beach in a sweet race boat and we turned a lot of heads. We had an innocent, but good time each day. After all, we were from Oral Roberts University. On the last day, just as we were headed back home, one of the engines completely stopped working. It would not turn over at all! I called my dad and guess what he told me to do? *Figure it out!*

Great! Just great! He did not come to my rescue or tell me what to do. The only thing I could do was slowly get back home using only one engine. This should have been a 30-minute journey under normal circumstances. This time it took somewhere around two hours to putt-putt home. It was so embarrassing to be going 5 mph in a speedboat, while everyone is passing you.

I also recall numerous other times when my car broke down, or I was faced with a sticky situation, and eventually I stopped calling dad each time to bail me out; as, I just figured out what to do for myself. This was very empowering, rather than always depending on my dad for the solution. His simple, three-word philosophy is forever ingrained in my psyche and has empowered me in numerous ways throughout my lifetime.

Today I truly believe I have the power to figure anything out. You may think how audacious of me, but I am not afraid to tackle anything, even if I know it is out of my league. Deep down, I know I am capable of utilizing the combination of my brainpower and the Holy Spirit. Therefore, I believe in me and the God in me. You must believe in yourself. We are made in His image and likeness. Do not ever underestimate your abilities. You are created in the God-class.

I recall the summer of 2014, while on a trip with Papa Myles. We were flying from Curacao to Medellin, Columbia in South America. I was given the privilege to sit toe-to-toe with him during each leg of the trip. *Thank you Carlos Seise for giving up your seat for me.* I took this opportunity to ask him many questions. One question was: "What are you doing before you speak in a session when you sit with your eyes closed?"

His response:

1. I am listening to the Holy Spirit and saying, "*You know what they need, so use me.*"

2. I am thinking about the content and the first statement I'm going to say - what's going on in their country; the issues going on.

3. I'm talking to myself - "*I can do this.*"

I was quite surprised to learn that even Dr. Myles Munroe had to remind himself that he could do this. You must believe that you can, and therefore, you will. Even if I do not know the solution at that moment, I know I am capable of eventually figuring it out. I might read an article, research online, ask people in the field, or read a book regarding a situation. I am always seeking. That's the key, never give up and never stop learning and asking questions. It doesn't matter if people tell you "no" or that it can't be done. In my mind, I never accept NO as an answer.

My son, Maverick, was a newborn in the late summer of 2012 when I had one of the worst seasons of my life. He was constantly screaming day and night for four months. I brought him to numerous pediatricians who said it was just colic; they sent me on my way with a recommendation for gas drops. I knew there was something else causing my baby to scream to the point of almost losing his voice, because of the strain on his vocal cords. I spent many days and nights researching online for answers. I changed my diet drastically, since I was nursing him. Imagine getting little or no sleep for months. It affected my mind to the point of having visions of driving my car off a cliff.

I cried out to God for the answer, and one night I found a recommendation on a baby blog for a book called *Colic Solved* by Bryan Vartabedian. The next morning, I dragged my screaming baby into the library and read the book in my car while sitting in the parking lot with Maverick screaming. Within ten minutes, I found the solution. Silent acid reflux was burning his esophagus. I knew it wasn't colic!

One of the solutions was nursing him on a certain side at an upright angle with him sleeping upright in a swing. This improved the situation by about 65%. It was also recommended to give the baby a stomach acid-blocker medication for severe cases. I went to a specialist who would not prescribe anything because Maverick was not vomiting blood. I was furious! None of the doctors would help and I was desperate for relief for both of us.

I went home and called a holistic, concierge pediatrician, whose waiting list I had been on since pregnancy. He happened to answer the phone and I cried as I asked if I had moved up from 12th in line on his waiting list and explained how none of the doctors could help us. He allowed me to come in the next day, as one of his seven children had the same problem and he understood and knew what to do. Serenity now! The answer was found along with the person to help us. Persistence was the key and I was very persistent; it took me four long months, constant research and asking for help from various people. I refused to accept 'no' as an answer from anyone, until I found what I was looking for.

Papa Myles often said, "An answer to your problem is usually found in a book somewhere on a shelf." I have found this to be true, time and time again. It may take some time as you may experience seasons of frustration. Regardless, be resolute that anything can be accomplished, if you stick with it. I think sometimes we give up too easily and are missing the powerful ingredient of tenacity. When I think of tenacity, I think of a bulldog. The word tenacity means *persistence, determination, perseverance, doggedness, strength of purpose.* Strength of purpose is when you know exactly what you were born to do, your heart is right and your face is set like flint (stone). This gives you full confidence that God has your back and therefore you become like a bulldog. For when you discover your purpose, passion and perseverance becomes fuel for your life vision.

God our Creator identifies himself with two animals, the lion and the eagle. Papa Myles would always teach about the qualities of these animals. Let us take a look at the lion's nature and attitude. The lion is considered the king of the animal kingdom, although he is not the fastest, largest, tallest or heaviest; he's not even smartest of the animal kingdom. The thing that makes him different, and therefore the king, is his mentality or attitude. Therefore, this is the most important quality a leader can posses; the right attitude, for it is separates leaders from the followers. This mentality makes the leader see situations differently. He looks at problems as opportunities to grow and benefit, rather than to defeat him. This is how a lion looks at an elephant. He is not intimidated by the size or strength of the elephant. He simply looks at the elephant and sees his next meal.

This attitude comes from a belief that you have what it takes, regardless of what it looks like in the natural. You cannot contrive this attitude; it must become part of your DNA, so that it becomes a natural instinct. All the odds may look like they are against you, but you know you have what it takes. The most important organ that God gave us was our brain. Then Jesus came to redeem us to receive the Holy Spirit again.

Are you kidding me? We have EVERYTHING we need in this lifetime. We must use them both in tandem. You must learn when not to listen to reason, and simply obey the principles of God. This will be addressed in detail later. You must know when to engage your God given intellect, creativity, and deductive reasoning. They work in tandem. You must use discernment. The more you use discernment in small areas, the easier it is to learn for the bigger tasks. This is why we need to teach children how to discern with their spirits.

I am grateful for this one ability that my mother instilled me in. As a teenager, I would ask to spend the night at someone's house, or go hang out with a group of friends. On one occasion, she asked me to imagine myself going with this group of friends to wherever it was we were going. Then she asked me if I had a 'sandpaper' feeling or a sense of peace about it. I did not have a complete peace about it, but rather a check in my spirit like something was not right, but I did not know what it was. So I responded, "sandpaper." I knew immediately I should not go. She did not make the decision for me at that moment. At age sixteen, my mom was training me to discern for myself. I made decisions based on the leading of the Holy Spirit in my spirit. She based this principle on Colossians 3:15 in the Amplified version:

> And let the peace (soul harmony which comes) from Christ rule (act as umpire continually) in your hearts [deciding and settling with finality all questions that arise in your minds, in that

peaceful state] to which as [members of Christ's] one body you were also called [to live]. AMP

We are to allow peace to dictate the decisions we make. An umpire is someone in baseball who calls the shots and arbitrates on the matters arising from the play. This is the role of the Holy Spirit to lead and guide you to all truth, regardless of whether you know the entire situation, or facts surrounding it. You might not know the future and all the factors or sometimes people do not give you the entire truth. However, you have the ability to make a decision based on the inner peace you do or do not have. In other words, you do not know why, but it just does not feel right.

I have carried this into my adulthood and it has made the biggest difference in my life. Now I am teaching this philosophy to my toddler son, Maverick. Anything, within reason and not in a state of danger, that he thinks he cannot work out, I will not come to his rescue. He is learning to stay with it until he gets the results he wants.

We recently moved into our new house that is a reflection of my husband Matthew's gifted architectural design. I planted my first garden and recently harvested our first little crop. I have organic beets, lettuce, tomatoes, basil and carrots. I wanted my toddler to experience pulling the carrots out of the ground. So I showed Maverick how to do it, and then encouraged him to try for himself. Rather than pulling straight up, he was pulling from the side and not able to get them out of the ground. I continued to coach him, "pull-up, pull, pull". He stopped and said, "Couldn't" in 'broken' English. I encouraged him to try again and when he did, the carrot still wouldn't budge, and he said, "Nope" and stopped. No way was I going to let him give up and watch me do it for him. So, again I coached him to "Try again - you can do it." On the third try, he did it! I exclaimed, "You did it!" I recorded this episode on my iPhone and every time he watches it, he is reminded that he did it.

I came from the religious community where for some reason were mostly led by our spirit and by every whim. On the other end of the spectrum, some people only operate with reasoning. There is a happy medium that is required for us to live effectively on the earth and still be connected to the Holy Spirit. I will never forget the day Papa Myles told me to write this book, he said, "Religious people have become too lazy; they don't think for themselves. We must utilize wisdom, knowledge and understanding as well as discernment from the Holy Spirit. My father used to tell me all the time, "God gave you a brain, use it."

> "Follow your heart, but take your brain with you."
> - Alfred Adler

We are the Ecclesia "called out ones", who are supposed to be bringing solutions to the systems of this world. They are supposed to come to us with their problems, as we provide relevant and practical solutions. Pharaoh asked Joseph where he got his wisdom from. He declared "Jehovah", and immediately Pharaoh proclaims we must serve his God Jehovah. Joseph knew what to do and structured a management program to prepare and survive for the famine Pharaoh saw in his dream from God.

I long to see more true agents of change solving community and national problems. This is possible; however, we must be trained and mentored with the correct mentality. Mentorship is a key factor and necessary for training how to properly influence and speak to the marketplace in their language. This is one of my primary assignments in life.

By now you are probably wondering, "Where is there a scripture to back up this principle?" You will not find one that says *'figure it out'* but I will point out that Paul did not say you would be transformed by the *removing* of your mind. He said, "Be transformed by the *renewing* of your mind." Your mind plays a huge role in ultimately who you become.

Renewing is a key word that we need to study. According to the Merriam-Webster's dictionary, it means *to make new or strong again; to begin again especially with more force or enthusiasm*. Therefore, we need to do some re-construction with our mind. We must consciously 'begin again' with a different mentality. The mentality is simply the original thinking of Adam in the garden. We must rediscover the original truth about ourselves and God. Once we know the truth we are set free from the mindsets of society. Truth is simply *original information*. This is my quest in life to understand the original information given by our Creator. When we discover the truth, the light bulb goes off. Our spirit immediately resounds with it. We don't need to be convinced of it. This is where we start to experience the abundant life. Jesus said, "I am the way to the truth that leads to life."[12] It can only be found in one place, the Holy Spirit. It is His job to reveal (unveil something that was always there) all truth to us.

> "I am the way to the truth that leads to life."
>
> - Jesus, original Aramaic

> "But when he, the Spirit of truth, comes, he will guide you into all the truth. He will not speak on his own; he will speak only what he hears, and he will tell you what is yet to come." (John 16:13)

Jesus is also referred to as the Spirit of truth. Not only does He reveal truth, He IS it! Many people receive the wrong information that causes them to make the wrong decisions; it is their wrong thinking in life. Once you discover the truth, you are to begin again, making your thinking new. Then you are a totally different person.

---

[12] John 14:6

"For as a man thinks, so is he."[13] Your thinking and beliefs make you who you are. Out of this thinking you make decisions every day. If your information is wrong, then your thinking is wrong. The renewing is a deliberate process that you facilitate. Nobody can do this for you.

I deliberately started this process on March 28, 2008, and never looked back. I heard a man from the Bahamas speak in a packed auditorium in Bradenton, Florida. I sat in the back of that room with a broken foot and tears streaming down my face, as I heard him speak about the original truth. He was not speaking about a religion. I have been a Christian since I was 5 years old, attended a Christian school with Bible study and scripture memorization daily. At age nine, my mother found Jesus and we started attending a Baptist church. Then by age 11, we were at the Assemblies of God where I received the Holy Spirit. My mom started saving a little bit of the grocery money that dad gave her each week so we could attend the South West Believers' Convention in Fort Worth, Texas hosted by Kenneth Copeland each year. We would pack our little suitcase and lunch cooler and make the three-day drive to Texas each year. My mom would save grocery money all year long, just so she could purchase tapes at the resource table at his conference. She would listen to them until the following year. We attended many conferences over my lifetime and I even taught 'College & Career' in my former church.

I recall a few times, we could not attend one of the conferences, because my father wasn't happy with us going for some reason. It seemed that he resented how much time mom spent at church, and for a while we did not attend at all and it was replaced with 'family day.' This only lasted about a year. I also remember when my dad cut the cord to the tape recorder while mom was listening to a Kenneth

---

[13] Proverbs 23:7

Copeland teaching. On the other hand, he was very respectful of God, for mom was surprised when dad found a glass of water on top of her Bible and made a fuss about it being placed there. I'm not exactly sure all that happened, because mom did not talk much about such things, and dad was the human vault. However, he attended an Easter Sunday service with us when I was in 5th grade. Now that was truly a miracle! I just believe dad did not want anything to do with organized religion, and I totally respected it and did not blame him at all.

Dr. Munroe's message in Florida was far more than all that I had ever heard as a Christian for 34 years of my life. It left me sitting with tears streaming down my face. I was hearing for the first time a message, stripped of all man's religion and traditions, revealing the original truth about who I am and God's Kingdom. I am a citizen of this Kingdom created to walk in dominion on the earth. He shared how Isaiah saw a child was born and a son was given and he was carrying a government on His shoulders.[14] WHAT? I was taught that Jesus brought a religion called Christianity when he came to earth. I thought that I was a soldier in the army of God, just singing to Him and waiting until Jesus returns. I thought I was just an unworthy sinner saved by grace.

When you hear the truth, your Spirit immediately recognizes it, attesting to it. I immediately knew that my search was over. I had found what I was looking for my entire life. My tears were a sigh of relief; my search was over. I found the pearl of great price. Religion was a substitute for it in my entire life. It blinded me, for I thought I had it – but, when I heard the truth, I knew it. A big weight was lifted. "His yoke is easy and burden truly is light".[15] I knew that scripture well, but I had never experienced it until that day.

---

[14] Isaiah 9:6
[15] Matthew 11:30

Religion is not a light burden for it does not fit, even though you try to make it happen by going thru the motions. People use religion to find a better world, meaning, and purpose. It has become a substitute for the Kingdom (government) of God. A substitute is dangerous - for you are accepting it as the original thing. Karl Marx said, "Religion is the opiate of the masses." An opiate is a drug that puts you in a state where you don't feel anything - you are numb. You are just going through the motions and swallowing what they are feeding you. Papa Myles say, "Christianity is the most effective tool of blindness." The gospel of the current church is nowhere close to the message of Jesus or His disciples. They had one message: the Kingdom of God has arrived!

What did Adam lose when he 'fell"? Once you *figure this out* you will discover what you are seeking. For, whatever he lost is the thing man is looking for. Whatever he lost is what we need; it is what Jesus the Christ redeemed for us. When you study what Jesus brought, you will discover what you lost. Did Adam lose or even 'fall' from heaven? I want you to think for yourself. When Adam disobeyed God and took a bite from the apple, what happened? He realized he was naked. God told him that he would surely die if he ate from the tree of the knowledge of good and evil. Did he physically die? No. Okay, so if he did not physically die and lived to be 930 years old, then what then does God consider death? Spiritual separation. The Spirit of God could strive not much more with man.[16] The Holy Spirit of God immediately left the man. When God drove the man from Eden ... He did not have to kill them. He said they would surely die. Adam needed the environment of God, the Holy Spirit to live. *This will be addressed later in detail.*

> "Religion is the opiate of the masses."
> - Karl Marx

---

[16] Genesis 6:3 NKJ

The Holy Spirit gives you power over circumstances in life. Power over sickness, weather, crops, animals, destruction. Power over everything on the earth, except over people. You will find this list and our mandate in Genesis 1:26-28.

"Then God said, 'Let us make mankind in our image, in our likeness, so that they may rule over the fish in the sea and the birds in the sky, over the livestock and all the wild animals, and over all the creatures that move along the ground.'

So God created mankind in his own image, in the image of God he created them; male and female he created them. God blessed them and said to them,

'Be fruitful and increase in number; fill the earth and subdue it. Rule over the fish in the sea and the birds in the sky and over every living creature that moves on the ground.' "

God gave us RULERSHIP over the fish, birds, livestock, wild animals and all the creatures on the ground. Then He commanded us to be fruitful, increase in number; fill the earth and SUBDUE it! In verse 28 the word "subdue" means *to overcome, bring under control.* We were created to subdue and rule over the earth. You will not find people in this list. The spirit of man cannot handle being opposed or ruled over. When we lost the Holy Spirit we lost dominion power. This is found in the word RULE from verse 26. In Hebrew' the word 'rule' is "radah" meaning *kingdom sovereignty, to reign and rule, authority over territory.* In Greek this word rule means "basileia": *kingdom, sovereignty and royal power.*" Are you starting to *figure out* the big picture now? You were born to rule the earth! You are a king who lost the kingdom! You lost the environment of God, the Holy Spirit.

Let us fast-forward to the New Testament. Jesus was going around Palestine proclaiming the good news of the Kingdom of God and its arrival. The Pharisees (religious rulers of the day) were trying to figure out when it would come. Jesus answered, "The coming of the kingdom of God is not something that can be observed, nor will people say, "Here it is," or "There it is," because **the kingdom of God is within you.**" (Luke 17:20-21). Adam was given a Kingdom, not a religion. Rulership, not rituals. Stewardship, not ownership. Dominion over the entire earth, not over mankind. This is what Adam lost and what every man on God's green earth is looking for. It is available to whosoever desires and accepts the Holy Spirit. Hopefully by now you are connecting the dots as to why the Bible refers to God as King of kings and Lord of lords.

Now, we will take it one more vital step further. Jesus' first statement of His ministry was "Repent, for the Kingdom of Heaven has arrived."[17] This is a paramount statement that few know the real meaning and power of. I was taught in religion that repentance was when I went to the altar at the front of the church and brought up all my sins, shortcomings, failures, and ask for forgiveness. I was to feel sorry, regret and pitiful for my actions and vowing to never behave that way again. However, this word has nothing to do with this religious act. In the New Testament, the word translated as 'repentance' is the Greek word μετάνοια (*metanoia*), "after/behind one's mind", which is a compound word of the preposition 'meta' (after, with), and the verb 'noeo' (to perceive, to think, the result of perceiving or observing). Metanoia is, therefore, primarily an after-thought, different from the former thought; a change of conduct, "change of mind and heart"[18] To paraphrase, Jesus was saying '*Change your thinking* for the Kingdom of God has arrived.' In other words, in order to operate and benefit from this Kingdom you must change your thinking with the original truth. REPENT for the KINGDOM of GOD has ARRIVED!

When you understand the original truth that you were created to dominate the earth and your circumstance, you think completely

---

[17] Matthew 4:17
[18] www.psychology.wikia.com

differently when faced with adversity. You know you were built for adversity and have the tenacity to make it through to the other side. However, if you still have religious thinking, you may think you are only built for the blessings in life. You unknowingly become part of the 'bless me club' and when adversity comes knocking at your door, you will not be equipped with the proper mentality and will be easily defeated or confused wondering, "What did I do wrong?"

A very important concept I must mention is that you cannot pour new wine into old wineskins.

"And no one pours new wine into old wineskins. Otherwise, the wine will burst the skins, and both the wine and the wineskins will be ruined. No, they pour new wine into new wineskins."[19]

This way of kingdom living and understanding can only be properly executed in your life if you have a new mindset. I have heard religious people try to teach the Kingdom out of zeal; they had not taken the time to shed the old way of thinking and it became mixed and very ineffective, and sometimes confusing to people.

There is a process the old wineskin has to go through for it to be able to receive new wine. Firstly, the old, tough wineskin has to be harshly beaten. Then, it must go through the process of soaking in water then beaten again; then, soaking over and over until it is soft and pliable enough to hold the new wine again. This is a metaphor for what your mind must go through in the process of transformation. It's a deliberate process only you can do. I think of it as deleting the software on the hard drive in order to download new software. The hard drive is your brain and the software is a new way of thinking; however, it is the original thinking that Adam had.

Recently, I came across a scientific experiment on a video that demonstrated this imperative principle perfectly called "The

---

[19] Mark 2:22

Backwards Brain Bicycle" by Smarter Every Day.[20] One day, some engineers created a backwards bike by changing one thing, the pivot on the front bike stem. This is what causes a normal bike to steer to the right when you turn the handlebar to the right. However, on a backwards bicycle, when the handlebars are turned to the right, the wheel turns instead to the left, and vice-versa.

Destin, a thirty-something year old man, rode this backwards bike every day for about 5 minutes. He didn't have a timeline or try to force his brain to re-learn how to ride a bike backwards. He just wanted to see how long it would take for his brain to naturally figure it out on its own. It took him 8 months to re-program the pattern of his brain to learn how to ride the backwards bike. However, for his six year old son, it only took two weeks.

This experiment not only depicts how much quicker it is for a child to re-learn something, but also how knowledge does not equal understanding. It points to how difficult it is to transition from the old patterns of thinking to different thinking in order to create a new behavior. Compared to an adult, the child's brain has much more neuro-plasticity, also known as brain plasticity, an umbrella term that encompasses both synaptic plasticity and non-synaptic plasticity—it refers to changes in neural pathways and synapses due to changes in behavior, environment, neural processes, thinking, and emotions.[21] This video truly confirms scientifically the principle behind the statement of Jesus, "Unless you change and become like little children, you will never enter the kingdom of heaven." (Matthew 18:10)

I cannot emphasize this critical step in understanding, processing and operating in the Kingdom. You simply have to

---

[20]www.YouTube.com "The Backwards Brain Bicycle - Smarter Every Day 133
[21] www.en.wikipedia.org

renew your way of thinking. Otherwise, life will be very difficult and frustrating. I may repeat myself a few times in this book on purpose. As humans, we need to have things re-emphasized and be reminded in order to change our mindset and gain understanding.

TAKE TIME TO THINK

I pray that you will utilize this philosophy when it comes to your own personal purpose in life. Everyone was born to solve a problem that humanity has. However, most people live life haphazardly and never discover why they are here. When you discover your purpose, it is the WHY. This is where your life vision comes into play. It is imperative that you write down HOW you are going to accomplish your WHY. That is where the most effective part of my *figure it out* philosophy has come into play. As I continue to train agents of change, and thereby changing the destiny of nations, I may not have all the solutions, but I know that I have the capability to eventually figure it out

> "Thinking is the hardest work there is, which is probably the reason why so few engage in it."
> -Henry Ford

through the process. I have found that majority of the time God will bring a person or a book into your life to connect the dots or a piece of the missing link. When God brings a new person in your life; study them. He is trying to show you something. Whoever you associate with becomes your future. Also, every time I have stepped out in faith by starting a program or project, I develop the answers and capabilities along the way. I think most people get stuck thinking they need to have everything in place before they start. That takes no faith whatsoever.

The programs and projects pertaining to my vision are far out of my league in the natural, but I inherently know I was built according to my purpose, and therefore, I have the capability to deliver. It is almost like faking it until you make it, except for the fact that I have the Holy Spirit leading me each step of the way. Therefore, I have the cutting edge advantage. I rely on Him to direct me, all while using my brain. It is a tandem operation. I do believe in creating your future and bringing it to you. Demanding it by activating steps of the vision. God is looking for people with childlike faith who have the belief that they can accomplish anything! It is almost like being naive or crazy enough to believe it. Except it works every time. I refuse to solely rely on my own understanding, or limited thinking. If it truly is something God has purposed for you to do, then He is obligated to help you with it. Read it for yourself:

"To man belong the plans of the heart, but from the LORD comes the reply of the tongue." (Proverbs 16:1)

Here is the Hebrew translation for this scripture "Man makes the plans, and God explains how it's going to be paid for."

WOW! What a finance program! Your job is to make the plans that God has created for you to execute. He then is obligated to finance them. God will not finance the bills you created, but He will finance the bills He created you to create. What a deal! The problem is that most people do not have a clear vision for their life. Herein lies the crutch; the resources cannot find your vision. They are looking for it.

Whether it is a personal, community or national challenge, understand that you truly have the ability to accomplish the obstacles at hand. Take these steps and attitude and apply them to your life, teach them to your children and you will get results, and therefore building confidence in your own God-given capabilities. Have the kind of attitude that says you have what it takes to *figure it out*.

IDEA GARDEN

Recently Matthew and I took Maverick to the Naples Botanical Gardens. As we walked the beautiful property, we came across an area called "Idea Garden". I thought that was a brilliant idea. A beautiful place in nature, to relax and just think.

I set aside time to think, contemplate and ask God questions. I cannot emphasize enough how important it is just to spend time thinking and listening. Papa Myles once said, "The ultimate prayer is meditation. The most effective prayer is listening." Too often, we spit out a list of things we need or problems we are having. However, the most effective prayer is listening to what the Holy Spirit is revealing to you. This is how you get results in life. Make it easier on yourself, spend more time listening and meditating than talking. I have found that when you are talking to God, that prayer primarily consists of claiming your rights, praying for others and your vision. This happens primarily when I am getting ready for work, driving in my car, or in my hot tub for a few minutes in the evening. Then, when my family is in bed, I sometimes read on my iPad or just spend time thinking, it's a lost art. Jesus spent hours each morning before starting his day. Historically, during his time, the days started around 5 a.m. This means he would rise to pray between 2-3 a.m. each day to receive his instructions from Father God. Then when the disciples awoke he would say, "Let's go to Judea or Galilee, etc…"

> "The ultimate prayer is meditation. The most effective prayer is listening."
> -Dr. Myles Munroe

Do you have a quiet place to go if for only 15 - 30 minutes at a time? A chair in your back yard, quiet time on your commute to work. Make time for yourself to sit and think, and see what happens. For me, I find nature is the most peaceful place to do this.

Ideas rule the world and can ultimately change it.

PRINCIPLE RECAP

1. You must believe in yourself and God in you.

2. Never give up or stop learning and asking questions.

3. When you discover your purpose, passion and perseverance becomes fuel for your life vision.

4. Strength of purpose is when you know exactly what you were born to do, your heart is right and your face is set like flint (stone).

5. Allow peace to dictate the decisions you make.

6. Utilize wisdom, knowledge and understanding as well as discernment from the Holy Spirit.

7. God gave you a brain use it.

8. Transformation happens by the renewing of your mind, not the removing of your mind.

9. Truth = original information.

10. God desires those with child like faith who believe they can accomplish anything.

11. Ideas rule the world and can ultimately change it.

Chapter 4

PAY ATTENTION

Life Lesson #2

"The only thing more expensive in life than education is ignorance."
- Benjamin Franklin

The second most repeated phrase in our family growing up was *'pay attention.'* Whether I was being taught how to drive a boat, a car, run equipment, soldering electrical, operating lathe machines or traveling, I was always reminded to pay attention. I had to pay attention to my surroundings while driving, pay attention to those around me, pay attention to my finances; all the little things. Pay attention to the big things. Just pay attention, be aware.

Now that I am an adult I still find myself paying attention. We cannot afford just to saunter through life going wherever the wind takes us. Life must be lived intentionally and deliberately. I try my best to remain very conscious of the big picture, which is my life. What is status of the world, our culture shifts, and the mindsets? What directions are the nations headed? What is my role in it? Am I on target with accomplishing my goals this year regarding my life assignment? It is only possible to measure this progress when you compare it with what you have written for your life vision. Where are we as the state of the Ecclesia? Where are we as a society ethically? What are our children observing and learning?

I live intentionally and am always cognizant of time; mine and the times we live in. One of the biggest irritants I have is wasting time. Therefore, I do not associate with people who might try to waste mine. Time and change are the only commodities that everyone has in common. Our lives consist of how we manage both elements. Simply put, TIME = LIFE. This is why I am adamant about creating the change I want to see. Being proactive with my life by the decisions I make, even on a daily basis. I am a product of the decisions I make and how I spend my time. This conviction was awakened in 2007 when my mom passed. She was only 55 years old and had fought a battle with cancer. That was my wake up call. I realized how short life is even at age 34. Then I did the math and determined I was only 20 years away from 55. That's when I promised to give God everything I am to make IT happen, but there was one condition: *I needed all of His resources.* I cannot tell you exactly what "it" was that I was going to make happen, but I was determined to MAKE IT HAPPEN! At that time, there was popular national furniture commercial on TV that played the song by a rock band named Queen, "I want it all and I want it now." Every time this commercial came on, I would jump up with my arms in the air singing "*I want it all and I want it now!*" This was the deep, deep cry of my heart and soul. When my mother passed, I had a small inheritance, so clearly I was not referring to money or material possessions.

There was something more that I was crying out for, but I had no idea what it was. Fast forward, eight months when I find myself sitting in an auditorium in Bradenton, Florida with a broken foot listening to a man from the Bahamas teaching about the Kingdom of God, I found what I was looking for. I found the only resource I was missing and I had demanded IT from God: and understanding of His *Kingdom.* My thirst was quenched with living water. Oh, it tasted so good! I no longer had the desire to go running from conference to conference or reading any more religious books. Immediately, after the service, I went to Dr. Myles Munroe's resource table and told the lady to "Give me every book, CD and DVD on the Kingdom of God. *I want it all and I want it now!*"

God had answered my prayer. I hobbled out to my car on crutches with bags of resources on the Kingdom of God, the happiest woman in the world! For the next six months I was consumed with listening to the CDs and repenting. I changed my mindset, transformed my thinking, and became a new person. The Holy Spirit cannot do this for you. Only YOU can transform your mind.

Perhaps you can understand why I am so adamant about my time. It is my life, and I am determined to give all that I am to my generation. Once you realize you have this responsibility to serve your gift to your generation, you become a slave to it. All I desire is to teach others what I have learned. I have become a slave to my gift of teaching. My gift is also my passion and therefore it brings me much joy each time I engage in it.

"I have seen the burden God has laid on the human race. He has made everything beautiful in its time. He has also set eternity in the human heart; yet[a] no one can fathom what God has done from beginning to end." (Ecclesiastes 3:10-11)

King Solomon is saying God matures everything in the time He gave it to be matured. You were given an assignment (burden) and a certain time to accomplish it when you are mature to complete it. You came out of eternity to complete an assignment within a certain period of time. You will be restless and unfulfilled until you discover what your purpose or life assignment is. I have discovered my purpose and am working on completing my assignment in the time that I have been given on this earth. I am determined not to waste one minute; time is a gift. Every day, week, month and year I have, I am grateful. I am constantly paying attention to the time I am given and the seasons I am in.

A person's days are determined; You have decreed the number of his months And have set limits he cannot exceed. So look away from him and let him alone, till he has put in his time like a hired laborer. (Job 14:5-6)

The Kingdom of God is not about measuring time by years, but by accomplishing your assignment. Jesus did not die old He died finished. He said, "IT is finished." What was finished? His assignment. This is when I realized what IT was I was referring to; my assignment. I promised to accomplish my assignment as long as I had the understanding and resources of the Kingdom of God. It took thirty-four years of seeking, perseverance, determination and finally demanding all the resources of God in order to discover THE Kingdom. You do not discover it haphazardly. Jesus says WHEN you SEEK, and you SEEK with ALL your HEART, you will FIND. It was not found while sitting in the local church in America or that Christian School I attended from ages 5 – 18, and it was not even found while attending Oral Roberts University. Now I understand these parables:

"The kingdom of heaven is like treasure hidden in a field. When a man found it, he hid it again, and then in his joy went and sold all he had and bought that field." (Matthew 13:44)

Jesus is describing the Kingdom of Heaven as being hidden. WHAT? Why is it hidden from us? The treasure was not sitting on top of the ground for the man to trip over. It was buried; therefore, you must diligently seek to find a buried treasure; do it with tenacity. God, who is everywhere, will only reveal Himself to those who want to see Him. David said, "If I go up to the heavens, you are there; if I make my bed in the depths, you are there." [22] There are many churches in each city, all over the world. However, in order to discover the Kingdom of God, you must seek it, and search for it

---

[22] Psalm 139:8

diligently. A lot of effort is not needed to find a church, you probably drive past one every day. However, He will only reveal Himself to those who are looking. James 4:8 says, "Come near to God and he will come near to you." God does that to protect His integrity. He will never give us something we do not desire. Otherwise, God would be lying to Himself. For instance, What if I tried to give you a glass of water to drink and you were not thirsty. You would say, 'No thanks.' What if I was persistent in forcing you to take the glass of water and insisted that you needed this water. You would feel that I was imposing myself on you and it would make you uncomfortable, for you are not even thirsty. I would be lying to myself if I were to give you something that you did not desire or even ask for. This is how religion imposes itself on people and tries to give them something they might not desire or ask for. This spirit goes as far back as the crusades.

Integrity means *one-with-self*. Who you are, what you do, and what you say, is ONE. The word 'integrity' is the same word used to describe God - HOLY. This is also why Jesus used parables when teaching to the multitudes. Parables protect the integrity of God's holiness. We must learn to respect the free will of each person, just as God does. No longer should we chase people down to impose our ideas or God on them. Only give people what they want to know. You will know when because they will ask questions, and it will remove the burden from you. I use to think it was my burden to save everyone I met. Then I learned to look at how Jesus did it. He taught in parables and the people probably thought they were nice stories. However, the hungry ones then came afterwards and asked questions that led Jesus to teach them in-depth and reveal the truths of God.

Jesus referring to the kingdom is demonstrated by using a man searching for something that is difficult to find, but priceless.

"Again, the kingdom of heaven is like a merchant looking for fine pearls. When he found one of great value, he went away and sold everything he had and bought it." (Matthew 13:46)

Discovering the original truth of the Kingdom and who you are makes you want to sell everything you have to get it; everything you need is found in this Kingdom. When I discovered the Kingdom, I gave away tons of religious books and music. They were my substitute, which no longer were of value. I discovered something of more value. The problem with religion is that we have converted the 'search' into 'the discovery'. The danger is we feel good when we have finished because we believe we have accomplished something by going through the experience of religion, yet never learning about the Kingdom.

PAY ATTENTION TO THE TIMES WE LIVE IN

I desire to be like the wise tribe of Issachar. A group of people who understood the signs of the times they lived in, the seasons of change, and they knew exactly what to do. (I Chronicles 12:32) They could comprehend, read and conceive the times they were in. They would tell the nation what to do. This statement implies three things: If you do not know the times in which we live then:

1. You will not know what to do.

2. You are probably doing the wrong thing.

3. If you know the seasons and the times, then you know what to do.

Some Christians become so holy and religious that they remove themselves from the media; having no televisions or cable in their dwelling. They do not realize the importance of having their eyes and ears open to the current events, watching documentaries regarding the state of different cultures, people, religious groups and nations.

The true Ecclesia cannot afford to live in a box with its head buried in the sand just sitting and waiting for Jesus to return.

THREE CAMPS (Mentalities) OF THE CHURCH

I have noticed three different mentalities or 'camps' of the 'church'.[23]

1. RAPTURE CAMP

This group of people has their hope in the coming rapture. They believe that the future is grim; and thus are in a holding pattern of 'neutral', just waiting for the Savior. Their hearts are projected toward heaven, therefore making them incapable of advancing the Kingdom of God on earth. Their thinking is "So what's the point since everything is going to be destroyed by war, earthquakes or God himself." This rapture camp tends to withdraw their involvement with society and changing the systems that operate it. My challenge with this mindset is that Jesus was very clear about our assignment and when the end would come in the book of Matthew.

> "Jesus answered: 'Watch out that no one deceives you. For many will come in my name, claiming, "I am the Messiah," and will deceive many. You will hear of wars and rumors of wars, but see to it that you are not alarmed. Such things must happen, but the end is still to come. Nation will rise against nation, and kingdom against kingdom. There will be famines and earthquakes in various places. All these are the beginning of birth-pains." (Matthew 24:4-8)

Jesus is saying all of these things must take place, but do not be alarmed - it is not the end yet, for this is just the beginning. Then in verse 14 He tells us what will determine the end:

---

[23]blog by John S. Garfield.

"And this gospel of the kingdom will be preached in the whole world as a testimony to all nations, and then the end will come."

Wait, you mean to tell me there is a message that determines the end? What message? The gospel of Calvary? The gospel of faith? The gospel of eternity? The gospel of the blood? As you can see there are many gospels, or good news, but there is a specific one to which he says will determine the end. THIS gospel of THE Kingdom will be preached and THEN the end will come.

Terrorists will not determine the end; not a nuclear war, and neither will an earthquake. These are all birthing pains. However, a very specific message determines the end. Jesus determined which gospel it would be, for he knew there would be many gospels being declared. Which gospel are you declaring? I have to admit, I used to belong to this camp of people. My mind was so heavenly fixated on all the events of the earth, that I was no earthly good. I had to change my thinking. I recall one of Jesus' prayers:

"My prayer is not that you take them out of the world but that you protect them from the evil one." (John 17:15)

His prayer is that we would remain in the world, and I was praying to leave! Where did I get this mindset from? I believe a lot of it came from songs I was singing in church and the sermons preached. We must start reading the Bible for ourselves, with the proper mindset so we can be delivered from any religious thinking. I cannot even listen to Christian contemporary music anymore. I do not want that kind of thinking to enter my mind. I make sure I guard my heart for I live my life according to my thinking.

"Above all else, guard your heart, for everything you do flows from it." (Proverbs 4:23)

The word *HEART* in the scriptures is the Hebrew word for *MIND*. Guard your mind, your thinking, for this determines how you function in life. Your life is built from your belief system, which comes from information you receive. So watch the things that you are downloading on your hard drive. Be careful to guard the wrong information from being planted as a seed into your mind.

2.   REVIVAL CAMP

The second camp consists of those who have their hope set on revival. This is largely a view of the prophetic movement. Historically, revivals have reminded us of God's ability to break out in power. They build their expectations around God's miracles and anticipation for revival power to break out. I have attended many revival tent crusades in my lifetime; now I have issues with this view.

> Jesus said "I am going to send you what my Father has promised; but stay in the city until you have been clothed with power from on high." (Luke 24:49)

Wait, did we receive the power or not? What are we waiting for? Our Heavenly Father has given us EVERYTHING that we need. He sent us the Holy Spirit, which gives us POWER! God has healed me instantly on many occasions; mononucleosis, a broken foot, headaches and a number of other issues I had. I have prayed over two female employees at my hotel, with both of them having pregnancy complications and fear of losing their babies. One lady's baby was forming in the fallopian tube and she asked me to pray for her. So, I put my hand on her stomach and said, "Baby move to the uterus now." I continued to pray for a healthy baby to form. That baby, Sophia is seven years old today. The other lady, who worked in my kitchen, had a healthy baby too.

I am not denying the power of miracles today. My issue is for those who are preoccupied with seeking after them. There was a time when a man with leprosy came to Jesus asking to be healed by saying:

> "Lord, if you are willing, you can make me clean.'

> Jesus reached out his hand and touched the man. 'I am willing,' he said. 'Be clean!' Immediately he was cleansed of his leprosy.

Then Jesus said to him, "See that you don't tell anyone." (Matthew 8:2-4)

WHAT? Jesus did not want the man to tell anyone that he was healed? A leper in that day was an outcast because he was so contagious. Leprosy is a chronic infection caused by bacteria that affects your nerves, respiratory tract and eyes. This may result in a lack of ability to feel pain and thus loss of parts of extremities due to repeated injuries.[24] However, this man was healed of this incurable disease in that day, and could return to his family and function in society again. That is a major shift! What could possibly motivate Jesus to tell him to keep his healing quiet? The answer is simple: **Jesus wanted to be known for His message, not the miracles**. He knew that many people would come as spectators and desiring to see a sign that he was the Messiah. So he did not want the miracles to overshadow the message. The religious people of that day, known as the Pharisees, demanded this of Him. They asked for a sign; however, Jesus refused and responded with

"A wicked and adulterous generation asks for a sign!" (Matthew 12:39)

3.   OCCUPY NOW CAMP

This is the third group of people that is starting to emerge. They understand that the Kingdom is within and are advancing it on the earth. Jesus commanded us to occupy until He comes. Another translation says, "Engage in business until I come." (Luke 19:13). He did not say wait until He comes, nor sing until He comes; or stockpile until He comes or sit in rooms for 24 hours praying and fasting until He comes. He's expecting a group of people, the Ecclesia, to be positioned in the present to make a difference in our generation and be the change the earth wants to see.

---

[24]www.en.wikipedia.org

There are many in this generation who desire to get it right. They are tired of corruption, lack of integrity, corporate greed and leadership without character. We need leaders who can solve the problems our nations are facing.

Now this next verse always baffled me when I had a religious mindset:

> "And he (Jesus) said to them, 'Truly I tell you, some who are standing here will not taste death before they see that the kingdom of God has come with power." (Mark 9:1)

I used to think that the kingdom would come back when Jesus returned or when we arrived to heaven. I really did not understand what this meant since I had never heard anyone teach this scripture. I thought- *but Jesus is dead and I do not see the Kingdom.* Then when I started understanding the Kingdom, it made perfect sense. After the cross, Jesus rose again and met up with the disciples for the first time. He breathed on them and said, "Receive the Holy Spirit"[25]. THAT'S IT!

Receive in Latin means to "take back". Take back the Holy Spirit. That is what Adam lost, the Spirit of God, which gives us dominion power! BOOM! Are you figuring it out yet? In essence, Jesus was saying to those standing with him, "*Listen guys, before you die you will see the Kingdom come back with its power!*" Understand what Jesus came to the earth to bring. That is what we lost. Dominion, power over our circumstances, and the earth. The kingdom is IN us. That is what Adam lost. This is what every man is looking for, POWER.

Perhaps you are saying, *I was also taught Jesus' purpose was to come to earth to die on the cross for our sins so you could go to heaven.* Let's read what Jesus said His purpose was:

---

[25] John 20:22

"Jesus replied, 'Let us go somewhere else– to the nearby villages– so that I can preach there also. <u>That is why I have come.</u>"[26]

Jesus was very clear about his purpose for being here, to preach a specific message about THE kingdom. He only had one message: Repent, for the Kingdom has arrived. Then he spoke in parables to the masses: the kingdom is like this and like that. As for the cross, it was a means to the end, but it was not the end itself. The end was to get the Holy Spirit back in us so we would no longer be victims of circumstance. We were created to rule and have dominion over the earth. We cannot afford to stay camped out at the cross any longer. Think about when Jesus rose from the dead. What did He talk about with his disciples? Did He discuss his persecution and death on the cross? Did He describe His three days in hell getting the keys of death, hell and the grave back? You think He would have told them about those three crazy days. Let us look at what He talked about during his last forty days on the earth before returning to His Father in Heaven.

"After his suffering, Jesus presented himself to them and gave convincing evidence that he was alive. He appeared over a period of forty days and spoke about the Kingdom of God." (Acts 1:3)

Whoa! There it is again - He spoke about the Kingdom of God. He did not mention the cross, hell, the suffering, defeating the devil, His blood or eternity. No, Jesus had only one message. Maybe you need to check your message. This is what Acts says next:

On one occasion, while he was eating with them, he gave them this command: 'Do not leave Jerusalem, but wait for the gift my Father promised, which you have heard me speak about. For

---

[26] Mark 1:38

John baptized with water, but in a few days you will be baptized with the Holy Spirit.'[27]

He kept telling His disciples to wait for the Holy Spirit and He called it the 'gift my Father promised.' This is what was promised us, for this is what Adam lost. This is your inheritance!

"Come, you who are blessed by my Father; take your inheritance, the kingdom prepared for you since the creation of the world." (Matthew 25:34)

I was taught that heaven was my inheritance. I had my ticket for fire insurance, protection from hell. It led me to believe I was just passing time waiting for the sweet by and by over in the sky. Then I found what I was looking for - this Kingdom that gives me power! This is so exciting! And I simply needed to just change my thinking. That process took six months and I never looked back. I will never stop renewing my mind, but I will never look back. If you glance back, look back; go back, you are not fit for His Kingdom.

"Jesus replied, 'No one who puts a hand to the plow and looks back is fit for service in the kingdom of God." (Luke 9:62)

The Kingdom is all or nothing. You are either hot or cold. There is no middle ground, no grey areas or complacency, but there is always a price to pay for something of value.

DO YOU HAVE THAT RARE INGREDIENT?

A key ingredient that God is looking for is called 'dedication'. He is not looking for loyalty, commitment, not even faithfulness. Loyal people can be loyal for the wrong reason. Committed and faithful people also can have ulterior motives for their commitment. However, dedicated people cancel all of their alternative plans and

---

[27] Acts 1:4-5

are dedicated to you. Jesus is looking for people who are 100% dedicated to Him and to fulfilling their purpose and life vision. I am reminded of the day that Jesus tested the motives of the 'bread and fish' Christians who were following Him.

"Jesus said to them, "Very truly I tell you, unless you eat the flesh of the Son of Man and drink his blood, you have no life in you." (John 6:53)

Jesus was testing the motives of those who followed Him. He was weeding out the serious ones who meant business and truly believed, and many turned away at that point. Then He turned to the twelve remaining and wanted to know whether they also wanted to leave. Their response set them apart from everyone else. 'There's nowhere else to go.' From this time many of his disciples turned back and no longer followed him.

"You do not want to leave too, do you?" Jesus asked the Twelve. Simon Peter answered him, "Lord, to whom shall we go? You have the words of eternal life. We have come to believe and to know that you are the Holy One of God." (John 6:67-69)

They had no other alternative. All other options were cancelled in their mind and this was it. Now that is real dedication; exactly what God is looking for. People who are completely dedicated with their face set like flint; not easily distracted or enticed by anything or anyone.

If you take care of God's business, He takes care of yours. A few months ago, as I started dedicating more time to my life vision and away from the daily grind of running a hotel, we were suddenly featured on one major national morning news broadcast with 4.8 million viewers.[28] The phone constantly rang at the hotel for an entire week! I just smiled, knowing God had set it all up. I did not have to

---

[28] www.TheWrap.com

try and make this happen. Besides, there was no way that I could afford such national marketing, but God did it in the blink of an eye.

I have been delegating more and have given more responsibility to the managers. Knowing that my vision would demand more of my time, I even replaced the general manager with one more experienced, knowing they were capable of handling the stress and problems of the hotel without having to rely on me to always make decisions.

This is just one example, so be aware of the things that God delights in doing for you when obedience is demonstrated in the vision He gave you to accomplish on the earth. You will be pleasantly surprised; simply amazed.

PRINCIPLE RECAP

1. You become a new person by changing your mindset and transforming your thinking.

2. You came out of eternity to complete an assignment within a certain period of time.

3. God only reveals himself to those who are seeking.

4. Everything you need is found in the Kingdom.

5. Jesus wanted to be known for His message, not the miracles.

Chapter 5

TELL IT LIKE IT IS

Life Lesson #3

"Our Character . . . is an omen of our destiny, and the more integrity we
have and keep, the simpler and nobler the destiny is likely to be."
-George Santayana

I learned this lesson while a young teen. It was engrained in me
from that same person who taught me the first two life lessons better
known as my dad. He would say, *"Tell it like it is"*, for it is better to
tell me the truth now than to get caught in a lie later. The
consequences would be much less. Again, I believed him.

Unfortunately, I had not yet learned this lesson in fourth grade
when my girlfriend spent the night at my house and left her ring in
my bedroom. I liked the ring and decided to keep it and even wore it
to school. I know that was not a bright idea at all! That week my
teacher approached me and asked if it was mine. My response was
'Yes'. She went on to say that my friend had recently lost a ring
identical to the one I was wearing. Now here's my chance to confess,
but I still denied it. I will never forget the feeling of lying in to
teacher's face. That weekend we were at McDonalds and I was in the
bathroom washing my hands and guess what went down the drain!
Yes, the ring I falsely claimed was mine. There I was staring down

the drain with no way of retrieving it. Trista Sue lost what she stole. What was the point? Now nobody could enjoy the ring.

From that day on I learned my lesson. *It does not pay to steal or lie about anything.* I would end up losing it one day anyways. Since I learned that lesson, if I find anything that someone left behind, no matter if in a store or a parking lot, I always turn it in if I did not see who lost it.

When I started working in the real world, I was quite shocked and appalled when adults would lie to me. I grew up in a bubble attending a Christian school, university, and church most of my life. So it took some time for me to understand that not everyone would tell the truth like I did. I was truly amazed to learn that adults would lie and steal. That one is still difficult for me to comprehend today. From the bartenders, to the managers, to my bookkeeper, who was staying at my house, because of personal challenges; living under my roof and stealing from me! What goes around comes around and I do not ever want to be in their shoes. I love the feeling of sleeping well at night without having a bad conscious for something I deliberately did. Growing older only revealed bigger tests. But when you are faithful in the little things, then God can trust you, because He knows you will be faithful with more.

I will never forget the day in March, 2014, when my husband came home from work and claimed to tell me some good news. Since he started his business around the same time as the BP Gulf oil spill (2010), he was eligible

> "Great men and women are not extraordinary people who do extraordinary things. They are ordinary people who do ordinary things with integrity."
> - Jayce O'Neal

for a large sum of money. A lawyer friend had contacted him and they went through his firm's financials to submit a claim. I just looked at Matthew and said "Oh, so the reason your firm did not make a lot of money the first year was because of the oil spill?" He looked at me and said, "No." I then responded, "Well then that is not your money." He paused and I watched to see his response. "You are right. I will not accept it." Of which my response was, "Good, I can stay married to you now." For in my mind I would not be equally yoked in my marriage if my husband was a thief. I was relieved knowing Matthew passed the character test on a settlement estimated to be $460,000. Yes, he declined a half a million dollars. The following morning Matthew sent this email to his lawyer friend:

> *I want to first start by thanking you for your suggestions and looking out for me in the most sincere way. I would also like your office to calculate any and all hours spent to date on this and please bill me. I have run into a bit of a moral roadblock. I have been so busy with this city park that this past evening was the first time I had the chance to talk to my wife about this.*

> *In summary, I am probably entitled to a settlement from the enormous brick wall we hit in the economy with my prior architectural firm PKStudios, where I was the "K". When I left there in the last part of 2009 to start my own firm, I had modest expectations to do business in Old Naples and focus on houses and commercial projects under my area of expertise. Since then, our firm popularity exploded and that is why we had such a revenue difference between 2010 and now. In good faith, I don't see how I could justify any of the income difference to be the fault of the oil spill. I was simply starting from scratch and was at the right place, with the right talent, selling the right product at the right time. I also had the backing of right standing, which I contribute to my success.*

> *As you probably know, Trista is an ordained minister and often teaches on living life in the right way. With this, we have taken a family approach to try to live life at the highest possible standard and gaining from something like this when not internally justified does not meet our vision.*

I hope you understand where we are coming from and I also hope you know this has absolutely nothing to do with you or your business. You are highly respected and I know you do everything you can to look after your client's best interest. I also like you very much as a friend and you will be the first that I call for any business related law services I require. With us and this particular situation, it is just something we would struggle with.

Thanks,
Matthew Kragh, AIA, NCARB

I was never as proud of him as in that moment. This was my response to him:

Matthew, God will honor you for operating with integrity -with more blessings in our lifetime than this settlement would have ever gotten you. You passed the test. I'm proud to be your wife!!!! - Trista Sue

I was so proud that Matthew passed the test; I even sent the email to my mentor, Papa Myles Munroe. This was his response:

Dear Trista,(Matthew),

It is a breath of fresh air and exceptional inspiration to read Matthew's letter and to see the integrity and Character it manifests. I am so proud of him and know that because he took such a high stand in the arena of business the Lord will open BIG DOORS in the next three month!! Get Ready! I personally want to give Matt my highest respect. You both make me proud associated with you and to see the ethical and moral foundations you are laying for Maverick. "He has great parents"!

God bless you both and I love you also.

In His Kingdom service,

Papa

Myles Munroe

The content of Papa's email shifted to '*the next generation.*' Most people do not understand that our decisions do affect the generations to follow. Some religious people would say, "Oh, you know that had to be God trying to bless you." or "I would have taken the money." I could not imagine taking money that did not rightfully belong to us. That is being deceitful. My world is very black and white, no gray area; those grey areas can get you in a lot of trouble down the road. Clearly, God was testing us. It was all a set up to see if He could trust us with more.

"Integrity is choosing your thoughts and actions based on values rather than personal gain."
-author unknown

But wait, that is not the end of the story about the claim. I recently learned that a few of Matthew's friends did submit start-up business claims with that same lawyer friend and were all denied. Therefore, we would NOT have received a settlement anyways, but now our intentions are proven to be clean before God.

Approximately three months after Papa Myles's email response, Matthew received a large job to develop with an entire island in the Caribbean. Specifically, the Bahamas. He said it was enough work to last him twenty years. Imagine a contract so large it could supply you with twenty years worth of work! Now, that's Kingdom. If we had taken the $460,000 then that is all we would have, and one day it would be depleted. Since we did not claim what did not rightfully belong to us, then God blessed us with a hundred times more wealth than that $460,000 would have ever provided.

That same year, I passed a $100,000 test when I declined some money that was rightfully due to me. However, the way it was presented to me would have been done under the table as in off the record. Therefore, I declined it. Matthew and I were both tested with large sums of money in 2014. I find that very interesting. It is obvious that God is up to something really big that will bring more glory to His Kingdom. Can you be trusted to pass the test?

Even Jesus himself was tested before His baptism when He was led by the Holy Spirit to the desert to be tested. God had to test His own son. When He is satisfied with our testing, then God gives without measure. Never trust anyone who has not passed the test or been tested. You are promoted in the Kingdom by testing. Like Papa Myles would say, "Do not become a proverb for people to talk about."

The authority sanctions your gift, but you still cannot be trusted. If God is going to use you greatly, you must pass these same three tests as Jesus did.

1. Appetites of the flesh including food, drink, drugs and sex.

2. Desire for fame, instant success.

3. Desire for power.

Some people continuously go through the same problems, because they still have not passed the test. Make it easy on yourself, pass the test the first time and get on with life.

In the midst of the 2009 recession in Southwest, Florida, I was pushing my husband to start his own architect firm. I understood a few principles; therefore, I was not concerned about the outcome of launching even when it was obvious that there was no business in the natural. I knew exactly what my husband's gift was, and based on the premise that his gift would make room for him, I knew regardless of the economy of America, he would succeed. Every day when Matthew came home from work I would push him for nine months to quit the firm where he was a twenty % partner. Finally, one day I asked, "What will it take to leave the firm?" He said, "When I don't receive a paycheck." I was so excited; immediately my prayer was that Matthew would not get paid. That day finally happened in August 2010, at which he gave his three-month notice. I then encouraged him to work at night with his own new clients. You see the problem Matthew had, was that he had signed a three year *no-compete* clause. Meaning, he could not take on any of the clients from that firm. In the natural there were no new clients to do work for in our city. After all, this was during the so-called recession, but it did not deter me, for I knew God could bring new clients out of nowhere.

Sure enough, Matthew had one new client that his old firm wanted nothing to do with. Matthew started with one very small job at night on our dining room table. This transition principle is found in Ecclesiastes 11:6

> "Sow your seed in the morning, and at evening let your hands not be idle, for you do not know which will succeed, whether this or that, or whether both will do equally well."

You go to work on the daily job that you were hired to do, and you work on your passion when you are not on the job. So if you have a day job, do it well and do not quit until your passion makes enough money. This is exactly what Matthew did. He was no overnight success, but he started with a one-man firm and now five years later, it is successful with an influential team of thirty-six people. He is featured in many design and home magazines, as well as on magazine covers.

Here is one more important factor to remember. When you are in your gifting, find your niche. Matthew is not only considered an architect, he has mastered his niche and is now known as "The Florida Architect."™ His design has a very distinctive look, and now he is transforming the look of Naples, according to all the articles and write-ups regarding his work.

In November 2009, Matthew found a small office and traded-out for rent by designing a small remodel of the building for the owner. He also needed to purchase a new computer and the expensive CAD software for drawings. His own parents were very concerned and worried about the risk Matthew was taking. But, when you understand Kingdom principles and how they work, once you activate them, you can be confident and sleep well at night. One day my father came to me and suggested that I should invest in Matthew. The hotel made a small investment in him for his hardware and software. So Matthew was in business with help from his community. That is the *power of community* and recognizing one's gift. A few years later, Matthew in return designed an interior and exterior renovation for the hotel, which far exceeds the original investment we made in him.

Back to *telling it like it is;* my hope is that you understand how important it is to be in right standing with our King. Now, you understand how imperative it is to walk in obedience and with integrity. Let me inform you of how Jesus simplified and summed up the Laws of God:

> "Do unto others as you would have done unto you." (Luke 6:31)

When people see you as trustworthy, honest, and upstanding in your dealings, they will notice you are different. You should be, you represent the Almighty King, and His culture is completely opposite of the world's culture. You are automatically required to live by a different set of standards and are 'set apart', not because of a preference or we are better than others, but because of conduct. So expect persecution, for none other than righteousness sake, and for choosing to take a stand and live right.

ONLY ONE TRUE ASSET

Our reputation is all that we have. Reputation is everything in my book. You can have fancy things, multiple homes, a big business or job title, but lacking in character. Some have big images, but no character. According to Genesis, what was the first thing that God gave man? It was HIS character, His image, His likeness, His being[29]. Man was given character before dominion. Character is necessary for dominion. Image has nothing to do with looking like God; it has to do with His nature, which is the very essence of God himself. Therefore, character is the most important component of who you are.

Character protects your gift and your life vision. It is when your public life and private life are the same, they line up. They are integral, which is where the word *integrity* is derived from. Who you are and what you say you are is one in the same. The world's leaders lead from their public life, then when their private life is revealed, we call them hypocrites. Kingdom citizens lead from their private life. Character is your private life whereas reputation is referring to your public life; it is what people think of you. Your goal in life is to make them one in the same.

> "Nearly all men can stand adversity. But if you want to test a man's character – give him power."
> -Abraham Lincoln

I will not associate with people who do not have character. If I did, people would associate my character level with theirs. I am not saying you should not talk to dishonest people, I am offering a word of caution about how you make it a habit to hang out with people who have a bad reputation. You cannot afford to have your Kingdom reputation tarnished knowing it is a reflection of Father God and will eventually affect your vision. The Holy Spirit cannot give you character, neither can you pray for it. It comes through many times of testing.

---

[29] Genesis 1:26

"...because we know that suffering produce perseverance; perseverance, character; and character, hope." (Romans 5:3b -4)

There it is! Character is a by-product of suffering, tests and trials. Many people try to avoid them; however you are to welcome them as friends. I know that sounds crazy, but its God doing something in you to get something out of you. He is refining you for a greater cause. You do not develop character in good times. As Papa Myles would say, "Whatever you are facing right now that you did not instigate is a classroom God created for you." The degree of your tests determines the degree of what God thinks about you and what He has in store for you. Trials come to develop you, not to destroy you. So understand this and decide to pass the tests. Like Papa Myles said numerous times, "You are only as strong as the test you survive." Never trust people who have no scars on their back. In other words, they have not been around long enough to know what it is like to be tested.

Papa Myles shared how the Romans being the most powerful empire at the time, used to make their swords. It was a process referred to as tempering. The Roman Empire was only as strong as the swords they used to overthrow their enemies. Therefore, it was imperative for the blacksmith to make the strongest swords. It was so important that their name be engraved on each sword that was made, and if any defect was detected on the battlefield, their life was as stake.   Here's the process of forging and tempering a sword.

The blade is carefully and evenly heated and then cooled slowly. The point of normalizing is to remove the stresses which may have built up within the body of the blade while it was being forged. During the forging process the blade might be heated and cooled differentially creating stress, some parts might be hammered more than others; some areas hammered enough to work harden. If these stresses are left in the blade they could affect the finishing and when it came time to heat treat the blade, the hardening and tempering might not be as even. Potentially, enough stress could be added that the blade would be weak in spots, weak enough that it could fail under enough stress.

As one of the last processes in fabricating a sword is quenching and tempering it. Quenching hardens the metal so it holds an edge longer but this also makes it very brittle. To restore some ductility and durability the sword is tempered.[30]

This is the same process you will go through in times of testing. You are put into the fire and then hammered out where there are areas of weakness. Next you are immersed in the cold water to harden and the process starts again in the fire. This makes the sword trustworthy when under pressure in the battlefield; it will not break. God does not want you to be destroyed or ill equipped when it is time for you to perform publicly. Testing is a process of removing the weaknesses of our lives, so when you are in the public eye, you will not yield to any temptations and can be completely trusted.

Trust is the foundation and source of character. Can God trust you? If you recall, He tested His own Son. He had to be proven for the weight of the vision. In other words, God is preparing you for what He's prepared for you. I will never forget one major test I faced when I was about to graduate from Oral Roberts University. I had changed my major in the middle of my junior year from business administration to health and exercise science. Therefore, when it was time to graduate in the summer of 1995, I needed to take one other class in order to graduate. This class, kinesiology, was only offered every two years and some fifteen students also needed that same class in order to graduate. The administration offered the class during the summer break as a three-week summer course and allowed us to graduate, as we would receive our diploma upon completing the class.

---

[30] www.en.wikipedia.org

The majority of the students who needed to take this class were on the baseball team, which one of them being my boyfriend at the time and, two other girls were in the class along with me. Kinesiology, also known as human kinetics, is the scientific study of human movement. Kinesiology addresses physiological, mechanical, and psychological mechanisms.[31] This subject can be very challenging and the book was very thick; the professor was known for giving tricky exams that consisted of questions that did not allow for simple deductive reasoning. You truly had to know your content. We covered a lot in a short time span, sometimes covering two chapters per day. In the afternoon, I would go to the local hospital and do my internship with my nights given to studying. When it was time for the final exam, I returned to my dorm from completing my internship job and noticed the entire baseball team sitting huddled in the lobby. My boyfriend approached me saying someone on the team had stolen the answer key to the final exam. He proceeded to tell me there was no way I could pass the final exam unless I studied the answer key. This final exam would make the difference between passing the class and graduating or having to return to take the class again. My college graduation was on the line.

At this time, I recalled my Spanish high school class where my best friend and I were caught cheating and we lied about it. I will never forget the feeling of lying to my teacher. And to this day, I do not remember anything I learned from that course. I clearly did not pass this test, and here I stand again faced with a test along with much higher stakes. So I had to make a decision as to what I would do. I immediately became very angry for I knew cheating was not an option. I went to my dorm room and started complaining to God. I told Him, "This isn't fair, I'm going to study all night and fail the exam and not be able to graduate while the cheaters get their diploma." I went and found two other girls. I told them the boys

---

[31] www.en.wikipedia.org

were all cheating; they were already aware of it and decided not to cheat. So us three girls studied hard that night for this big final exam that would determine our destiny for the summer.

The next morning, we assembled in the professor's classroom. When he arrived in the room, he announced, "Somebody stole the answer key to the test, therefore, I don't know the answers to the test. So, today the final exam is going to be three essay questions." The girls and I had glowing faces; we were so excited because of how much we had studied to be prepared. You should have seen the look on all the boys' faces. So guess who graduated? Only the three girls who studied, and decided not to cheat.

That was a HUGE lesson I learned that day as well as my boyfriend and the other boys in the class. This is a classic example of the consequences of taking shortcuts in life. You end up wasting time, energy and money with the long run of ending right back where you started. I do not know about you, but I don't have time for that. I would rather pass the test the first time and get on with my life.

NEVER TAKE THE LONG-CUT

For one reason or another, too many people do not want to take the time to figure things out the proper and ethical way. They prefer taking short-cuts. All short cuts are evil and are actually considered long-cuts. This means people are not always willing to pay the price, put the time and energy in to do it right. It will take longer to get the results they wanted rather than if they would have done it right the first time around. Usually, with long-cuts there are repercussions. Regardless, there is always a price to pay, sooner or later, for anything you want in life.

Although everyone around you is taking the short-cuts in life, I promise, if you make the right decisions the first time around, you will be far better off in the long-run. I think of how impressed Jesus was with Nathanael when He saw him approaching and said of him, "Here truly is an Israelite in whom there is no deceit."[32] Another translation says a *man of complete integrity* (NLT). This is what I want people to think of me. Let it be, "Hey, there's Trista, she's so pure." That is one of the highest compliments anyone can pay me. The leaders in my team tease me about being as *pure as the driven snow.* People know I want nothing from them. If I need your assistance or advice, I will make it very plain.

Most people you meet are looking for an angle or a way to benefit from you financially. Whether to sell you something, give them something, or sign up for their multi-level-marketing program. I get it all the time, especially being in the hotel business. I am not sure where people learn this from. Neither of my parents operated like this. They were both straight shooters and told us exactly like it was; straight talk. I will never forget the day I was in the van with Papa Myles and Mama Ruth in the summer of 2014 in Peru. Nobody was talking and he was just sitting in silence looking out the window. He said, "Trista." I responded, "Yes, sir." I was expecting an instruction, as we were headed to the conference he was speaking at. He said, "I love you." I was stunned and did not know exactly how to respond. I said, "Awhhh, thanks I love you both too." *Mama Ruth was sitting next to me; I did not want to exclude her.* He continued, "I love you. You are a good girl." Those were the two most beautiful statements I have ever heard! Those words made me feel so validated. He said he loved me more times than my own father, who told me once at age twenty-five. He also knew I wanted nothing from him, not to benefit from his relationship for my own promotion. I had no agenda except to observe and learn from him. In my mind, my mentor paid me the highest compliment possible. I did not need him to tell me how anointed or gifted I am or that I am a great businesswoman.

---

[32] John 1:47

Over the years I have observed so many people use Papa Myles to promote their business, or sell their products and build their ministry. When you are legitimate in your purpose you do not need to use others to promote yourself or your ministry. Just go about your business and do what God called you to do. Promotion comes from God. Relax, work hard on your life vision and be yourself.

I recall traveling with Papa Myles in Medellin, Columbia in the summer of 2014. We were in a car doing a bit of sightseeing one afternoon between sessions. While discussing fasting, I asked questions about his personal life regarding this practice. I remember being amazed at his response, for he truly set the bar so high in so many areas of his life. I said, "Thank you Papa for setting the bar so high." There is a price he paid to be who he was, which most people did not realize. There was also another reason why I decided to submit to him as a mentee, not only for his message, but his character and unwavering compromise, which is hard to find anywhere. Let's strive to set the bar a little higher and be the light to a dark world as we properly represent our King.

PRINCIPLE RECAP

1. Pass the test the first time.

2. When you understand Kingdom principles and how they work you can activate them and be confident in the results.

3. Character is necessary for dominion.

4. Character protects your gift and your life vision.

5. You are only as strong as the test you survive.

6. God has to prepare you for what He's prepared for you.

7. Your purpose will promote you.

"The credit belongs to those actually in the arena, whose faces are marred by dust and sweat and blood; who strive valiantly; who err; who at the worst, if they fail, fail while daring greatly, so that their place shall never be with those cold and timid souls who neither know victory nor defeat."

-*Theodore Roosevelt*

Me with my dad at 'Harvey Heights' circa 1975 assisting him with our new pool he was building.

My mom standing in front of dad's first rotary well rig he built.

Me driving my sister around on my motor-cycle, around age 5.

Mom and I hiking at Rocky Mountain National Park for her 50th birthday in 2001.

The weekend of March 2008 when I first heard the message of the Kingdom of God.

With Papa Myles during the Kingdom Training
Seminar in Nassau, Bahamas, 2014.

Traveling with Dr. Myles Munroe during the
summer of 2014. He was writing his final book.

The Kragh Family - Matthew, Maverick, and Trista Sue

Chapter 6

SHOW ME YOUR FRUIT

Life Lesson #4

"Therefore I tell you that the kingdom of God will be taken away from you and given to a people who will produce its fruit." (Matthew 21:43)
- Jesus

Show Me Your Fruit was chosen as one of my key life lesson because it is a Kingdom mandate throughout the Gospels. I had never heard it emphasized in the church in my earlier Christian life, but the Bible clearly unveils Jesus' Kingdom ministry here on earth and how He was 'righteousness' conscious rather than sin conscious. This lesson is my largest focus at this point in life now that I now understand Kingdom principles.

My daily concern is whether my energy is managed well and produces Kingdom fruit. I refuse to spend my time and energy on a project, a board or a business that is getting little results. You must know when to walk away from a project and know when to keep pressing until you get the measured results that you desired.

Knowing your purpose in life will eliminate many unnecessary programs, projects and meetings. I only engage in projects that support my life vision. This makes it very easy for me to say "no" to a lot of things rather than getting caught up in projects that maybe good but not right. It will also eliminate you from helping others fulfill their purpose while neglecting your own. But I will always take the time to help others regarding their purpose or vision. I believe in being a sounding board for others when it comes to making important life decisions.

Let us look first at the management mandate given by God to Adam and referred to by Jesus, so we can see how to manage the things God has already set before us. Genesis chapter 2 it states it this way:

> "Now no shrub had yet appeared on the earth and no plant had yet sprung up, for the Lord God had not sent rain on the earth and there was no one to work the ground," [33]

God had not even allowed the plants to appear on the earth until He created a man to manage them. That is very serious. The earth needed a manager and accordingly God will even withhold the rain when there is no manager. Then in verse 15 it states:

> "The Lord God took the man and put him in the Garden of Eden to work it and take care of it."

Adam's purpose was to manage and take care of the garden. That is our responsibility on the earth. We are to manage it and the resources. We have been given dominion and stewardship over the earth. For the Bible says, "The earth is the LORD's, and everything in it, the world, and all who live in it;" Psalms 24:1. God is the owner but He has given us stewardship, management over His creation. This is our mandate. Now let us take a look at Jesus' view on this topic in Matthew 25.

---

[33] Genesis 2:8

> "Again, it will be like a man going on a journey, who called his servants and entrusted his wealth to them. To one he gave five bags of gold, to another two bags, and to another one bag, each according to his ability. Then he went on his journey."[34]

Jesus acknowledges how God entrusted His resources to mankind and then sits back and watches what he does with it. The main assignment given to mankind is earth's management of its resources. I find it interesting how three people were given three different amounts of money. The reason being is the *amount given is equal to their ability to manage it*. God is aware of everybody's different ability to manage, so He can only release the resources accordingly. This is good news to me, for my ability is not that of someone else and I understand that God will never give me more than I can manage. This gives me full confidence that whatever is entrusted to my care I am quite capable of managing it.

> "The man who had received five bags of gold went at once and put his money to work and gained five bags more. So also, the one with two bags of gold gained two more. But the man who had received one bag went off, dug a hole in the ground and hid his master's money."[35]

Note the first man who receives five bags of gold *put his money to work*. It does not say "he went to work". This is a very crucial principle. In the Kingdom you do not work for money, it works for you. Otherwise you will be a slave to it and it will elude you. If you recall, this is one of the two masters every man serves: *God or money*. The third man went off and dug a hole for his money. In other words he did nothing with what was given to him. Now let's look at

---

[34] Matthew 25:14-15
[35] Matthew 25:16-18

what happens when the owner returns. God asks us to give an account of what we did with what we were given to manage.

> "After a long time the master of those servants returned and settled accounts with them. The man who had received five bags of gold brought the other five. 'Master,' he said, 'you entrusted me with five bags of gold. See, I have gained five more.'
>
> "His master replied, 'Well done, good and faithful servant! You have been faithful with a few things; I will put you in charge of many things. Come and share your master's happiness!'[36]

The man who doubled what was given to him was rewarded and given much more to be steward over. This is the key principle that I want you to remember: A good manager always adds value. I am extremely conscious of this in my daily life including my house, the hotel I manage, my car, my time and relationships. God will only give to effective

> "Money is merely a means to a greater purpose, not the purpose itself."
> -Penman Ghadimi

managers. You can also see here that proper management attracts resources to your life. Management is mans measure of success on the earth. When I graduated from Oral Roberts University in 1995, after working in the grapefruit grove, I moved to Naples, Florida. The cost of living is very high here and I was making very little money to be able to live in Naples. My father's philosophy towards his children is he expects twice as much from us and pays us half as much. So when it came time for me to find a place to live, I realized renting an apartment was above my means. So naturally I thought of moving into a trailer park, just like what I grew up in. In checking on

---

[36] Matthew 25:19-21

the various sites, I discovered they were for persons over fifty-five years old and I had just reached age twenty-two. Finally I found a trailer park that offered a family section and the lot was only $300 dollars a month. This I could afford. I went to my father and asked him if he had any job site work trailers that he was not using and to my joy he did. I was very excited as I had my first little spot to call my home. Though it was only 60 x 20 foot wide, it was my home. My father owned it, and he gave me complete stewardship over it.

I found a small lot with a concrete driveway already poured, so we moved the trailer there and I immediately set up camp. Sod was purchased, a small sprinkler system was installed and I planted some flowers. Next was the inside that got some attention. I installed cute pink drapes, bought a new sofa cover for the worn-out sofa that came with the trailer, and I got a new tablecloth to cover the card table that served as my dining table. I was set and proud of my new so-called 'pad' in the trailer park. It was the one trailer that stood out with a manicured grass yard and a trailer that was also clean on the outside. I managed my little yard and trailer to the best of my ability; the weeds were pulled; the grass cut and I even pressure washed my trailer, all by myself. It was my home for three or four years while managing it to the best of my ability.

Eventually I moved into a rented condo, which I also managed to the best of my ability. When I returned my father's work trailer, it was in better shape than when I received it. I applied the principle of adding value. Eventually I moved into a house, which I also managed to the very best my ability. I hope you see the pattern here that shows how I started out in a small trailer but I managed well. Also since I first moved to Naples there was one neighborhood that I had always wanted to live in located close to downtown with many little canals to live on. I eventually ended up there howbeit, it took me fifteen years and now I am enjoying the fruit of my management. I went through the process. Never try to bypass the process. No matter how tempting the shortcuts may be, go through the process. Trust the process.

So many people try to bypass the process by prayer only. Prayer does not cancel your management mandate. We make this mistake only to our own detriment in life. So many are praying to win the lottery or for that 'big check' to come in the mail. Through this parable it is clear that God will only give to you according to what you can manage. So we must never be confused thinking that prayer can override principles. This is so prevalent in the church. On the other hand, answered prayer is regulated by your capacity to manage. So you must never pray beyond your ability to manage. Now, let us finish the parable:

> "The man with two bags of gold also came. 'Master,' he said, 'you entrusted me with two bags of gold; see, I have gained two more.'
>
> "His master replied, 'Well done, good and faithful servant! You have been faithful with a few things; I will put you in charge of many things. Come and share your master's happiness!'[37]

The man who was given only two bags of gold received the same benefits as the man with five bags. His doubled and he was given stewardship over more resources. Now we will take a look at what happened to the man who did nothing with what he was given to manage.

> "Then the man who had received one bag of gold came. 'Master,' he said, 'I knew that you are a hard man, harvesting where you have not sown and gathering where you have not scattered seed. So I was afraid and went out and hid your gold in the ground. See, here is what belongs to you."

---

[37] Matthew 25:22-23

"His master replied, 'you wicked, lazy servant! So you knew that I harvest where I have not sown and gather where I have not scattered seed? Well then, you should have put my money on deposit with the bankers, so that when I returned I would have received it back with interest.' "

" 'So take the bag of gold from him and give it to the one who has ten bags. For whoever has will be given more and they will have an abundance. Whoever does not have, even what they have will be taken from them. And throw that worthless servant outside, into the darkness, where there will be weeping and gnashing of teeth.' "[38]

Jesus called him wicked and lazy because he did nothing with what he was given. Then Jesus takes it one step further by taking away the little the man had and throwing him into the darkness where there was weeping and gnashing of teeth. That is how the Bible describes Hell. Can you imagine at the end of your life giving an account to God for what you did with what He gave you and not doing anything? I will let you come to you own conclusions with that.

I suggest that you discover your purpose and execute it through your life vision.

I do not want you to think that Jesus only referred to this important principle one time. Here is another parable of the "Shrewd manager" found in Luke chapter 16.

Jesus told his disciples:

"There was a rich man whose manager was accused of wasting his possessions. So he called him in and asked him, 'What is this

---

[38] Matthew 25:24-30

I hear about you? **Give an account of your management**, because you cannot be manager any longer.'

"The manager said to him, 'What shall I do now? My master is taking away my job. I'm not strong enough to dig, and I'm ashamed to beg— I know what I'll do so that, when I lose my job here, people will welcome me into their houses.'

"So he called in each one of his master's debtors. He asked the first, 'How much do you owe my master?'

" 'Nine hundred gallons of olive oil,' he replied.

"The manager told him, 'Take your bill, sit down quickly, and make it four hundred and fifty.'

"Then he asked the second, 'and how much do you owe?'

" 'A thousand bushels of wheat,' he replied.

"He told him, 'Take your bill and make it eight hundred.'

"The master commended the dishonest manager because he had acted shrewdly. For the people of this world are more shrewd in dealing with their own kind than are the people of the light. I tell you, use worldly wealth to gain friends for yourselves, so that when it is gone, you will be welcomed into eternal dwellings.

"Whoever can be trusted with very little can also be trusted with much, and whoever is dishonest with very little will also be dishonest with much. So if you have not been trustworthy in handling worldly wealth, who will trust you with true riches? And if you have not been trustworthy with someone else's property, who will give you property of your own?"[39]

---

[39] Luke 16:1-12

Many principles are found in this parable. The manager who wasted the owner's possessions was asked to give an account of his stewardship and subsequently fired. The manager then acted shrewdly by reducing the amount of debt everyone owed. He was commended for this act. He thought of a way to keep his job and came up with a plan.

Jesus then tells us, the people of light (knowledge) to act shrewdly also. The word shrewd is defined as: *having or showing an ability to understand things and to make good judgments: mentally sharp or clever*[40]. Jesus says we need to think this way too. This is not an evil word, but simply reminding us to use our brain and think.

Then Jesus instructs us to use worldly wealth to gain friends. What He is saying is to use the world and study them because we are naive. Be their friends; get into politics, business and sports to learn from their systems. They know how to manage better than the church does. Dr. Myles Munroe would say many times "You learn more from a business person than a religious man begging for money."

Sadly I have often regretted hiring a religious person for a job. I try not to generalize and give the benefit of the doubt for many I meet; however this has been my overall experience in the work place. Whether it was a position at the hotel or someone hired to do electrical work. They seem to lack diligence and excellence. We represent the King and must do everything with high standards. This is engrained in my subconscious. I am not perfect, but I do the very best of my ability knowing God will honor that.

This principle is reinforced once again by Jesus. If you are not faithful in managing the little you have, God will not give you more.

---

[40] www.Merriam-webster.com

Do not be naive in thinking that prayer or fasting will override this principle. He even adds the word *riches* here, which refer to *abundantly supplied resources.*[41] We must understand the use of the resources for the vision. They are not for us to consume for our own personal ambition.

I have been asked by many in my retreats to state the difference between true vision and personal ambition, and the answer is simple: Who benefits from it? If you are the one benefiting from the resources then that is ambition. If others also benefit from the resources that is true vision.

The final scripture in this parable is where Jesus says if you cannot be trustworthy and manage somebody else's property then who in their right mind would give you a property of your own? Certainly nobody, including God himself. Here's where my trailer comes in as an example. I managed the trailer my father owned and I gave it back to him in better condition than when I received it. And now fifteen years later, I live in a beautiful home that my husband, an architect, and I recently moved into that is a day and night management job. If I did not manage the small trailer that I started with when I moved to Naples clearly there is no way I could manage our newly built and expansive home.

The definition of management is the *effective, efficient, correct and timely use of another person's property and resources for the purpose for which they were delegated within you to producing the expected added value*[42].

I know these principles seem fairly elementary, but many people completely miss the boat in their lives because they have negated this

---

[41] www.dictionary.reference.com
[42] "Overcoming Crisis" – Dr. Myles Munroe

principle. When I was given the hotel to manage in 1995, it was a Comfort Inn with 101 rooms painted a Pepto-Bismol pink. It was hideous, and frankly running a Comfort Inn was nothing glamorous. I made a lot of mistakes and I learned a lot of valuable lessons along the way. However I have managed that hotel to the best of my ability even though I had no formal education in hospitality management. My father taught me to *figure it out* and that is exactly what I did. This way of thinking is automatic for me. I innately believe I have the capability to do anything asked of me. You must believe in yourself.

I recall the net profit the first year was $35,000. The last two decades I have done a number of renovations, and eventually became an independent boutique hotel. Today I am operating with only 85 rooms. I have added banquet and meeting space, a small spa, fitness center, and a kitchen; and we make approximately $1 million in yearly net profit. I have added value to the concrete block that I was given stewardship over on this waterfront corner lot in downtown Naples, Florida. I also have been able to financially support many of my father's businesses every year, especially during the recession when he was on the brink of losing everything. In my mind I have managed this business as unto God as well as unto my father, the owner on paper.

> "The two most important days in your life are: the day you are born and the day you figure out why."
> - Mark Twain

INNOVATE

This is an area that is very interesting and extremely important to me. For God did not give Adam a table and a chair. He gave trees for lumber and an imagination capable of making anything that he could

107

dream of. This is the spirit of innovation. There are a number of ways to do any one thing. Sometimes we get stuck in only one way of doing "business as usual". We must not be afraid to think outside the box and approach situations through the lens of a different pair of glasses.

I learned this valuable lesson in 2009 when we were in the midst of recession in Southwest Florida. I had just returned from a conference in Bradenton where Dr. Munroe was teaching on his new book *"Overcoming Crisis."* He taught many principles regarding innovation, change, and vision, which I took notes like a crazy woman and came back inspired. This was also the time I started nagging my husband to launch his own company. Yes, I nagged him for nine months.

One day the week after the conference in Bradenton, Florida, I was looking at our inventory for February, as it is the busiest month of the entire year and business was dead. The phones were not ringing nor were any reservations coming in via the emails or fax machine. In South Florida our high season only last three to four months from Christmas to Easter. The revenue we make during this time makes it possible to pay the mortgage, payroll, utilities and all the bills for the remainder of the year. And here we sat in the middle of the season with little activity. I knew we would be in trouble if something did not change. I instantly remembered the principle of innovation I had just learned that weekend from Papa Myles. Sitting at my desk I stared at my computer screen and looked at my room inventory. I then asked the Holy Spirit, "Help me see what I cannot see." And I kept looking at my inventory. I had just learned that "There is nothing new under the sun[43]" and innovation is simply a way of combining old things in a new way. Within five minutes I saw

---

[43] Ecclesiastes 1:9

something I had never seen before in those fifteen years of operating the hotel. I have been trained to sell rooms a certain way, according to their view. So my rates were tiered accordingly. I had my city view rooms, then my next tier up are for the water view rooms, and then the water view luxury rooms on the top floor. For example, during high season I would sell a city-view room for $195, a water-view room for $250 and a luxury water-view for $295. As I sat looking at my inventory it dawned on me that there was always a little demand for a room with two double beds. EUREKA! So I decided to tier my rooms another step further according to the room type. I had the idea to sell my City-view with two double beds for a special recession rate of $99. This is unheard of in Naples, Florida in the middle of a high season with a downtown location for $99 as this is 50% off normal rates. However, these rooms were sitting empty and 100% of something is better than 100% of nothing. I therefore priced the city-view king beds somewhere around $149, and I priced the water view with two double beds around $175 and bay view rooms with a king bed somewhere around $199. Instead of offering three tiered rates I was offering six.

I then instructed my staff to change the rates accordingly in all the third-party online systems (Expedia, Orbitz, Travelocity...etc.) By the time it was uploaded into the system it was around 5 o'clock in the afternoon, we all went home and when we arrived to work the next morning we were inundated with reservations for the next four days, and we could hardly keep up with the demand. I had to hire more staff to keep up with the hotel occupancy. That was the best year in the history of the hotel regardless of being in the midst of a recession.

My job was to simply study my existing resources and combine them in a new way. I did not have to spend more money on marketing; all I had to do was look and see. See what I could not see before. The success of this one idea made a way for me to travel all over the world and teach business principles to Muslims and Hindus from all walks of life. People are looking to have their problems solved, not be proselytize to. I was taught how to teach Kingdom principles in a way that was not offensive. We must be taught the art of become all things to all men, so we may reach a few[44]. I was taught this art by Papa Myles. Now, I am teaching it to others. This is why you find me in Lebanon, India, Turkey, and Indonesia teaching in places where it may be difficult for a preacher to go. I do not teach in the churches either. Most of the time it is in a hotel meeting room or conference center. This is why a Muslim will come. A church building is a huge barrier to most of the world as it is. We must revisit the history of the original ecclesia and the ministry of Jesus. A synagogue was a community center in the days of the New Testament. The Greek word for synagogue is *assembly*[45]. This is where we can be most effective, out in the midst of the world. The most ineffective time is when religious people are huddled together on a Sunday morning. My focus is reaching and training those who are tired of religion and its rituals and desire to make a difference before they die, to become an agent of change.

I must not negate the other stories Jesus spoke of regarding management and adding value. This is the parable of the ten Minas found in Luke. While they were listening to this, he went on to tell them a parable, because he was near Jerusalem and the people thought that the Kingdom of God was going to appear at once.

> "He said: "A man of noble birth went to a distant country to have himself appointed king and then to return. So he called ten of his servants and gave them ten minas.[a] '**Put this money to work**,' he said, 'until I come back.'

---

[44] 1 Corinthians 9:22
[45] www.Merriam-webster.com

"But his subjects hated him and sent a delegation after him to say, 'We don't want this man to be our king.'

"He was made king, however, and returned home. Then he sent for the servants to whom he had given the money, in order to find out **what they had gained with it.**

"The first one came and said, 'Sir, your mina has earned ten more.'

" 'Well done, my good servant!' his master replied. 'Because you have been trustworthy in a very small matter, take charge of ten cities.'

"The second came and said, 'Sir, your mina has earned five more.'

"His master answered, 'You take charge of five cities.'

"Then another servant came and said, 'Sir, here is your mina; I have kept it laid away in a piece of cloth. I was afraid of you, because you are a hard man. You take out what you did not put in and reap what you did not sow.'

"His master replied, 'I will judge you by your own words, you wicked servant! You knew, did you, that I am a hard man, taking out what I did not put in, and reaping what I did not sow? Why then didn't't you put my money on deposit, so that when I came back, I could have collected it with interest?'

"Then he said to those standing by, 'Take his mina away from him and give it to the one who has ten minas.'

" 'Sir,' they said, 'he already has ten!'

"He replied, 'I tell you that to everyone who has, more will be given, but as for the one who has nothing, even what they have will be taken away. But those enemies of mine who did not want me to be king over them—bring them here and kill them in front of me.' "[46]

In the beginning of this story Jesus is referring to a noble who was made King in a distant land and then returned home. Many even protested him becoming the king. Sounds similar to Jesus himself, no? Notice once again, he told his ten servants to *put the money to work.* Then when he returned, he demanded to see what the servants had *gained* with the money. I think you see the pattern here. We must manage and add value to everything under our care. We will give an account at the end of our lives for what we do with what we are given. I believe this also includes our gifts and talents. I must finish with this final point. Jesus was referring to seeds that were sown in different people when they heard the message of the Kingdom. Then he says:

> "Others, like seed sown on good soil, hear the word, accept it, and produce a crop—some thirty, some sixty, some a hundred times what was sown."[47]

He clearly expects people to produce a crop, or fruit. He states they will produce different quantities, according to their capability. Now I want to refer you to a scripture I never heard anyone teach in all my years.

> "Therefore I tell you that the kingdom of God will be taken away from you and given to a people who will produce its fruit."[48]

Jesus is saying that the Kingdom of God will be taken from anyone who does not produce anything. The word for fruit is the

---

[46] Luke 19:11-17
[47] Mark 4:20
[48] Matthew 21:43

Greek word *karpos,* meaning *action, result, gain or profit.*[49] He is expecting action, results and increase. This is true with anything that God has created. Everything reproduces after itself naturally. Therefore, He expects the same of each individual in His Kingdom. I do not want you to be overwhelmed, just aware of God's expectations of us. I believe the simple key for producing fruit in the Kingdom is found in one word: obedience. This is the most important word in the Kingdom. Do not forget it.

KISS PRINCIPLE - *Keep It Short & Simple*

I am now going to give you the main ingredient to producing fruit. It is found in Luke 10.

> "Martha, Martha," the Lord answered, "You are worried and upset about many things, but few things are needed—or indeed only one."[50]

That is it! This tells me a few things that greatly simplified my life:

- We are concerned over so many things in life.

- Only a few things are truly necessary in life.

- Most of the time it can be reduced to one thing.

Here we see Jesus is referring to Mary sitting at his feet listening to His teaching. This is the 'seeking the Kingdom part of the formula.' I applied this to my life vision. I have spent years executing and refining it since 2010. Now I have narrowed it down to one vision statement. Everything I do, every project, every book, every teaching, every retreat I host, every webinar is supporting this one

---

[49] www.biblehub.com
[50] Luke 10:41-42

objective of my life. Rather than doing multiple things, which I am capable, I am doing a few projects that support one final goal for my life. When my life is stripped away of everything, it all comes down to this. I cannot imagine doing anything else. I know exactly what I was born to do and why. I understand why God made my temperament a certain way, why I get angry at certain things, why my upbringing was the way it was, as well as who my parents were. I needed both mentality extremes of my parents in my life to nurture me for my purpose.

Everything in my past benefits and supports my future. When Papa Myles passed in November 2014, I spent months meditating and reflecting to get to the bottom line of the rest of my life. I had to wrap my head around a lot of different factors and get advice and insight from my mentor and husband. It was quite a transition, but it all came down to what I had originally written in my vision, which became extremely refined and clearer. Therefore, I have spent the entire year of 2015 preparing, planning and initiating it. God has even provided a dedicated administrator for the vision, for whom it would not be possible to accomplish what He wants done on the earth without her. Once you get serious and dedicated to your purpose just watch God respond with the resources to support it.

I understand what Jesus meant when He said "Whoever finds their life will lose it, and whoever loses their life for my sake will find it."[51] Trust me when I say that I can easily live a very comfortable life in Naples, raise my children, travel and eventually retire. That just does not cut it for me. That is not living, it is ordinary mundane existing. In my mind we are just getting started with our true-life assignments. It is only the beginning. I know my burden of responsibility; I will give an account and thus, bear fruit with my life.

---

[51] Matthew 10:39

Eliminate projects that are a distraction and are not conducive to your vision. Take the time to sit down and think. Then simplify your life and stay focused.

PRINCIPLE RECAP

1. Knowing your purpose eliminates involvement in unnecessary programs, projects and meetings.

2. God has given you dominion and stewardship over the earth; therefore, you are to manage it and its resources.

3. Money is a resource in the Kingdom; it works for you.

4. Good managers always add value.

5. Proper management attracts resources to your life.

6. Managing your resources ensures success on earth.

7. Don't take the short-cut or bypass the process.

8. Prayer does not cancel your management mandate.

9. Prayer does not override principles.

10. Ambition only benefits you, however true vision benefits others.

11. Management is the effective, efficient, correct and timely use of another person's property and resources for the purpose for which they were delegated within you to producing the expected added value.

12. The spirit of innovation is evident by the number of ways to do any one thing. It is simply a way of combining old things in a new way.

13. Manage and add value to what God has entrusted you with.

14. Obedience is a key to producing fruit in the Kingdom.

15. God expects action, results and increase.

16. Your past benefits and supports your future.

17. Take the time to sit down and think. Then simplify your life and stay focused.

Chapter 7

DREAM BIG, BUILD SMALL

Life Lesson #5

"Big things have small beginnings."
- Prometheus

Do you have a vision? If so, what steps have you taken in executing it? Getting to your place of destiny requires going all out, and you have to be willing to go full speed ahead with a determination to give it all you've got. That goes beyond just attending church prayer meetings. It takes more than prayer to create the change you envision. Most of my life was spent in the church waiting and praying. I never understood why my family members and others were not really getting the results they wanted in life.

I have spent the past six years mentoring and training leaders in my community. I always encourage everyone to fulfill their purpose in life by documenting their life vision on paper. This is the most effective way to solidify why you are here and how you are going to accomplish your purpose. For until you have written it out on paper, you have not committed yourself to life, and there is no road map to fulfill your destiny. During this time I became frustrated wondering why so many people who came to me sharing their purpose and dreams, never even attempted to fulfill them. They knew what they were and were always discussing them, but over time I saw nothing happening. There was no fruit in their lives. You know how big Jesus is on bearing fruit. Even towards the end of his life assignment, He made a profound statement: "I have brought you glory on earth by finishing the work you gave me to do." (John 17:4)

Jesus was clear on his purpose and accomplishing it within thirty-three years. When your purpose is done, you can leave. He also stated that giving God glory had to do with accomplishing his purpose. Jesus did not mention singing or praying or fasting gives God glory, but completing the work He was sent to do. That is how you glorify God with your life.

I spent most of my life with the belief that somehow God would make it all work out for me. I just trusted that He would lead me somewhere, somehow. Unfortunately, I never spent time planning or initiating anything specific, until I understood how vision works. It wasn't until 2009 when I joined Dr. Myles Munroe's mentorship program where my final assignment for level three was to document my life vision. After finishing his book, "*The Principles and Power of Vision*," I wondered how I could have spent thirty-five years of my life not being guided by a vision. It suddenly became so clear how people perish for a lack of vision.[52] Meaning, they throw away restraint, living haphazardly without a clear focus.

> "For those determined to fly, having no wings is just a little detail."
> -Princess Sassy Pants & Co.™

Since 2010 I have never felt more alive and fulfilled as I do accomplishing my vision. I now can track the progress of my assignment by referring to my vision. This eliminates complacency in life or competition with others. I have a deep desire to see others feel this same way. This is why I spend much time teaching and hosting

---

[52] Proverbs 29:18

retreats, so others can find their purpose and write their vision. However, when I did not see these individuals living out their vision I started trying to understand why. Why do some people I have been training actually live out their dreams and others do not ever seem to reach that point. The power of vision works for me and I am no different. God is no respecter of persons. After asking many people questions and research, I came to a conclusion. It is nothing that I am doing wrong in my teaching style or communication efforts. I realized it came down to one vital ingredient:

INITIATIVE

> "The most effective way to do it, is to do it."
> -Amelia Earhart

Only you can develop initiative. It is a characteristic that nobody can give you, including the Holy Spirit. I am always impressed by anyone who works at my hotel with this ingredient. The majority of individuals with this ingredient have been promoted to management positions, even if they do not have the required experience. I appreciate this quality so much, which I find usually coincides with their positive attitude; they look for solutions rather than excuses. I would rather promote someone with initiative who may not have the experience than to train an experienced person to get it. Even if they do not solve the problems effectively, at least they try and I give them props for their efforts. I become cross-eyed when I encounter people who stand around waiting to be told what to do. They are not using their God-given intellect. They are not looking around to see what they can do to add value, instead they may see how much little effort they put forth and still do enough to get a pay check. People like this usually change jobs numerous times in their life.

Here is where I find the "dream big, build small" theory extremely helpful. It gives you the freedom to dream as big as possible, yet without being too overwhelmed to actually complete the expansive vision you see. Once you dream as big as your imagination can fathom, then start back at the beginning with the first stepping-stone to accomplish the task. The biggest hindrance to most people in this process is they limit their imagination, perhaps because of finances or they have been conditioned away from thinking too big. We must not let anyone hinder our gift of imagination or creativity and thereby our life assignment. It should be bigger than you, for if it is a true vision you will need to rely on God to bring it to fruition. On the other hand, He needs you on the earth in order to produce His will by accomplishing your life purpose. It's a beautiful partnership.

Let's take an in-depth look at the word initiative. It is an *introductory act or step; leading action; readiness and ability in initiating action.*[53] It does not mean you know exactly what to do in every situation;

> "They didn't know it was impossible, so they did it"
> -Mark Twain

however it is the small action step forward in doing something. Usually what I have found is that each time I take a small step forward in an unknown territory, I will know at some point what the next step is, but only after I have taken the first one. At times the perfect contact is made, or I find the solution in a book on my bookshelf, or in a person. This is why I do not have to know exactly what I am doing each time I aim to accomplish a project or idea. Almost every time it becomes much more amazing then I would have ever dreamed, but I always made that first initial step. It may be in calling someone who knows someone who is an expert in that area, or connecting with someone who has the same desire. By the time it is all said and done, you look like a pro! You look like you knew exactly what you were doing and people will come to you and

---

[53] www.Dictionary.reference.com May 2015

ask, "How did you do that?" Most of the time when I am asked this, I just shrug and say, "I don't know, I just did it and I had no clue what I was doing, but I *figured it out*." People do not believe me, but it is true. If I have an idea that will accomplish a piece of the vision then it does not take long for me to start the introductory step. It is that small step forward in the direction you want to go. Then you will find that it takes on a life of its own. I liken it to the domino effect. Once you initiate that first domino, it starts toppling the next and the next. Pretty soon you have advanced so much until it is amazing how it expands and forms into something so beautiful. However, I only recommend you do this if the project lines up with your vision, otherwise you will waste time, money, and resources. You may be successful, but I would rather be successful in doing the right thing, rather than a good thing.

True success in the Kingdom of God is accomplishing your life assignment. This is why we cannot compete or compare ourselves to others. Everyone's life assignment is unique. You can only compare yourself to the progression of your own life assignment.

PLANNING - THE KEY TO INITIATING CHANGE

A key element in initiating change, a project or an idea is planning. When I learned this important process during Dr. Myles Munroe's mentorship program, everything in my life began changing. I was seeing progress and results. I started planning my way towards my vision. It is so simple, but I was never formally taught this. I discovered I was created to live life, not for life to live me.

Planning is the most important principle of success in life. Where in the Bible are we instructed to live by hope? We are instructed to live by faith.[54] The highest form of faith is preparation, planning, and

---

[54] Hebrews 10:31

expectation. This gets God's attention. Without a plan, time and change will ruin your life. God gave you the mental and intellectual facilities to facilitate the creative process of planning for change. This is what separates us from the animal kingdom.

My husband Matthew is a successful architect in our city where his influence and talent are reaching beyond our nation. With each client he sits and hears the vision they have for their desired project. It may be residential, commercial development or an entire community or island. Then he sits down and designs on CAD software, and then produces a blueprint, which can be seen on paper. This is the plan that must be given to the builder of the project.

> "The best way to predict the future is to invent it."
> - Abraham Lincoln

You cannot start a vision without a plan in his field. You cannot implement a project with the idea trapped in the client's head. It must be conceptualized on paper. This process is what has made my husband successful. People fly from all over the nation to give their vision to my Matthew so he can put the plan on paper. He is very good at conceptualizing their vision and producing a final design concept on paper.

You see how important a plan is. It is actually finishing before you get started. Planning is more work than the actual work itself. It requires taking time to stop and think. I believe this is where we have missed it. Stop, think, plan and then initiate the steps in the plan.

As Abraham Lincoln stated "The best way to predict the future is to invent it." I am living proof of this. You can demand your future now. In religion I was always waiting and praying. Stop asking God for a plan, you give Him a plan. For what I have experienced, when you give God a plan now you are engaging Him and are truly committed to life. "To humans belong the plans of the heart, but from the Lord comes the proper answer of the tongue." (Proverbs 16:1)

This clearly demonstrates where the plans come from: man's heart (mind). You are responsible for planning, which controls time and change. From your heart (mind) comes the ideas and creative process utilizing the gift of imagination. Then the best part: God will explain how the plan will be executed and financed. He will lead and guide you each step of the way and He also provides the resources. "In his heart a man plans his course, but the Lord determines his steps." (Proverbs 16:9)

God's responsibility is to guide you each step of the way and to finance it. This explains why so many people are broke and going nowhere. They have never planned their way to their destination. Now for all of you who may second-guess yourselves and your ideas, let me help you a bit.

"The thoughts of the righteous are right..." (Proverbs 12:5a)

If you are in right standing with the King then God will speak to you through your thoughts. If your heart is right then your thoughts are right. This is how you know God's will. It is as close as your deepest thoughts and desires. Stop second-guessing yourself always wondering and hesitating. However, I always recommend you bring your ideas to a trusted Godly expert, mentor or spouse. They can confirm what you are thinking along with the proper timing of things.

"Plans fail for lack of counsel, but with many advisers they succeed." (Proverbs 15:22)

Your responsibility is to make sure you are planning according to your purpose.

"Many are the plans of a man's heart, but it is the Lords purpose that prevails." (Proverbs 19:21)

> "The only place where your dream becomes impossible is in your own thinking."
> - Robert Schuller

Purpose is the destiny that started your journey. Your purpose gives birth to the plans. When you plan according to your purpose you cannot go wrong. However, I must mention to you that plans are not a prison. They can take a detour at times, which is the process of the Lord leading and guiding you each step of the way. There are many ways to get to a destination. You put the destination in your GPS and let the Holy Spirit give you the best route.

"My ways are higher than yours and my thoughts than your thoughts."[55]

It takes faith to live like this, but my friend now you are truly living. I did a little bit of research to discover some of the reasons why people do not take initiative. Here are a few theories I discovered on www.Dialogueworks.com.

1. Bound Rationality

They do not see beyond what they know. If a situation arises that is beyond their expertise or experience they have a hard time perceiving what is going on. People can be functionally blinded by their own experience and expertise.

I believe every human has the ability to *figure it out*, one way or another. This may be through meeting an expert or researching alternatives. I believe wholeheartedly in the principle "seek and you shall find".[56] The problem is that YOU must do the seeking and too many people do not take the time or have the initiative to look.

---

[55] Isaiah 55:9
[56] Matthew 7:7

2. Lack of capability

When confronted with a task or situation entirely outside their experience or expertise, people lack the knowledge to do what is asked. They just do not know how, and they might not even know what questions to ask in order to begin to grasp what is required. They may not understand the directions they are given. Or they might not be willing to run the risk of being perceived as stupid or inept, so they do not dare to ask you to clarify questions that might reveal their ignorance or ineptitude. They say nothing and complete the task incorrectly or not at all.

Sometimes when people are asked to do something they have never done before, they feel like they are being asked to walk out of the light and into the darkness of the unknown. This is an uncomfortable place to be, especially if they believe there are negative consequences for a wrong decision or action.

God is looking for people who take initiative. I am a very simple person known for asking people to talk simply to me when giving instructions. I do not feel stupid, I am just seeking clarity. Therefore I am always asking questions so I can walk away knowing what is required of me. I would rather be perceived as 'simple' in the beginning, than a fool at the end when I have wasted my time doing something with the wrong results.

3. Task overload

Others have so much on their plate that they simply cannot process one more assignment. These overworked people will often shut down or refuse to take on anything else; keeping solely to the tasks they have been assigned. Unfortunately, they often do this without telling anyone about their overload, so the challenge or the new assignment goes unaddressed.

My advice is simple tell the truth. Perhaps you have too much going on to take on the task. Do not commit to something knowing you cannot accomplish it in the allotted time frame. I have done this many times. People appreciate your honesty, rather than the disappointment at the end when there is nothing to show for the assignment.

4. Ignorance by Convenience

Shades of this dynamic may be present in all of the other dynamics. I have heard people say they found "not knowing" to be quite convenient. "Ignorance is bliss." In other words, I cannot be held accountable for what I do not know *how* to do or what I simply *don't* do. These "ignorant" folks actually go so far as to say that they would rather accept the consequences for failing to act at all, rather than face the consequences of doing the wrong thing.

5. Management "Search and Rescue"

You may be surprised to learn that for some people, simple inaction seems to be a viable strategy. These people indicated that in their experience, if they do nothing, then someone else (usually a manager) will step in and do it for them. Managers, take note that this style of "rescue management" teaches people that they do not need to be accountable, while it robs them of the experience of learning from their mistakes. Those whom you rescue in this way do not learn to think critically or develop viable solutions to their challenges. They simply assume someone else will pick up the slack.

6. Execution over Innovation

Some people are so task-driven that they are more concerned about working through their list of to-do than about taking on a new task that may have no clear path to solution. Their list has become more important than the skill of figuring out a new solution.

God is looking for people who have this vital ingredient of initiative. I think of the great leader, Moses. He was standing by the Red Sea and declared:

"Do not be afraid. Stand firm and you will see the deliverance the Lord will bring you today. The Egyptians you see today you will never see again. The Lord will fight for you; you need only to be still." Then the Lord said to Moses, "Why are you crying out to me? Tell the Israelites to move on. Raise your staff and stretch out your hand over the sea to divide the water so that the Israelites can go through the sea on dry ground." (Exodus 14:13-16)

Moses initiated action by a statement. He did not wait for the Lord to tell him what to do. He declared what God would do, although he did not know how it would be done. Then God told Him the exact step to take. This is the perfect example of initiative. It truly is living by faith, but with works. For faith without works is dead [57]. The highest form of preparation is faith. You want to get God's attention? Live by faith.

Jesus was very clear that unless we come like a child we will never enter, understand or be able to operate in the Kingdom of God. The only way to make it in this life on earth effectively

> "That's the real trouble with the world, too many people grow up."
> -Walt Disney

is to stay connected with heaven. This truly takes child-like faith. I have encountered religious people with titles, degrees and many followers, who cannot comprehend the Kingdom of God. You have to lower yourself to the simplicity of child-like thinking and let go of your theology. You must be willing to re-learn and renew your mindset. When you come to God as a child He will reveal things to you.

That reminds me of an encounter I had in 2010. I will never forget a well-known religious figure in the Dallas, Texas area who

---

[57] James 2:26

attended a retreat I was hosting at my hotel. Twenty pastors spent a week relaxing and conducting meetings for their global organization. One sunny afternoon I was sitting, chatting with my pastor friend from Haiti and a friend whom I was mentoring. Out of nowhere two pastors approached our table; the one from Dallas with a large church pointed his fingers at me and said sternly, "What do you know that I don't know about the Kingdom of God." I was shocked, for I hardly knew the man and never spoke to him except in casual greetings. I suggested that they sit down and join us so we could engage in a conversation regarding his question. He refused and said,

> "If you are not willing to learn, no one can help you. If you are determined to learn, no one can stop you."
> -unkown author

"Tell me in thirty seconds what you know." I immediately knew that he really was not interested in learning anything. Instead, he wanted to know what in the world could a young hotelier know that he, with his theology degree and large church, did not know. So I summarized it in thirty seconds, and he responded by turning on his heels in a huff and walked away. I was amazed at his hostility and attitude. However, his friend came to me quietly the next morning asking if I had any teaching resources on the Kingdom of God.

> At that time Jesus said, "I praise you, Father, Lord of heaven and earth, because you have hidden these things from the wise and learned, and revealed them to little children. Yes, Father, for this is what you were pleased to do."[58]

It is impossible to function properly in the Kingdom of God without a child-like mentality. **It requires 100% trust and faith to operate effectively.** This I believe is why so many people struggle

---

[58] Luke 10:21

and get frustrated. **They bring their old way of thinking in the Kingdom. It simply will not function properly.**

Initiate the impossible. Whatever you decide to do according to your life vision, go all out and never look back. People may think you are crazy, but I think you need just a little bit of crazy in you to live by faith. When you are being rooted in your purpose, you do not need or care for the approval of people. Set your mind to do what you were born to do, regardless of the opinions of others. I remember reading this scripture in college in the Message Bible.

> "I'm not going to walk around on eggshells worrying about what small-minded people might say; I'm going to stride free and easy, knowing what our large-minded Master has already said." (I Corinthians 10:29 Message)

Paul was referring to eating certain foods at a guest's house. However, this is a great way to think. Ever since then I took this scripture to heart and am living by it. As long as I am doing what God sent me to do on earth, there is no need to worry about anyone else's approval. You were born to make a difference. You must be different in order to go against the masses. You must not be easily swayed by the opinions or gossip of others. If you are alone this does not mean you are wrong; you might be the only one right. It is about whether you believe in the truth. Conviction outlasts popular opinion.

This brings me to the meaning of my son's name, Maverick: *an unorthodox or independent-minded person. Someone who refuses to play by the rules. He/she isn't scared to cross the line of conformity, but their unorthodox tactics get results![59]* I am training him to think for himself and not to go with the flow of the mindset of our present culture.

We are required to obey the laws, but must break the rules that

---

[59] www.Urbandictionary.com

society has engrained in us. The Kingdom goes against the grain; the norm of doing things. This describes almost the entire Bible. Do not live another day for others. Live for God. Live for your purpose. Make a difference and initiate the change you want to see. It will affect more people than you realize. This is not about you. It is about everyone God wants to reach through you. I cannot imagine where I would be if I never attended that meeting where Papa Myles was speaking in Bradenton, Florida in 2008. Many lives have been changed because of this message I am carrying. It is about what you are carrying, it's not just for you. Do not be a generational thief. You will give an account for what you are carrying. This message of the Kingdom needs your gift to be shared with others. That is the vehicle for God to use. However, if you do not know your gift or your purpose then what vehicle do you have to utilize?

Jesus shared a powerful parable regarding the various types of people that want to do something for God.

He said to another man, "Follow me."

But he replied, "Lord, first let me go and bury my father."

Jesus said to him, "Let the dead bury their own dead, but you go and proclaim the kingdom of God."

Still another said, "I will follow you, Lord; but first let me go back and say goodbye to my family."

Jesus replied, "No one who puts a hand to the plow and looks back is fit for service in the kingdom of God."[60]

'Not fit' means not *of a suitable quality, standard, or type to meet the required purpose; of no good use; not appropriate; unqualified or incompetent for function*[61]. It's also defined another way: *being in such a state as to be or*

---

[60] Luke 9:59-62
[61] www.Dictionary.reference.com

seem ready to do or suffer something; adapted to the environment so as to be capable of surviving.[62]

In other words, you are not suitable for God to use you. You will not survive, for there will be hard times ahead. There is no room for double-mindedness, distractions or excuses. **God is looking for dedicated, focused individuals with the right mentality.**

As spouses and parents, our priorities are clearly our families, raising them properly and providing for them. However, we must take our life assignment seriously and be dedicated to the service of the Kingdom of God through our life vision. God has given each of us a responsibility according to our ability.

My philosophy is once you have decided to do something, be lion-hearted. Without risk there is no reward. I have had failures and invested in projects that did not succeed. However, I have no regrets. I would have regretted not trying, and would have never known the outcome. Some may see these ventures as "failures," but I simply see them as classroom lessons in life. I believe they ultimately taught me lessons, in which I will avoid future, more detrimental 'failures' or lessons. They have made me wiser and keener to whom I partner with. I have learned that it does not matter if they are Christian or a Kingdom citizen, can they manage money? Have they done their homework? Are they experts in their field? For I have also learned that not every good opportunity is right. It is only right if it lines up with my vision.

Take the first step in executing your vision. Do your research, plan, ask for advice and then go all out, full speed ahead. It is all or nothing, no in between. Give it all you've got and have the mentality that you can succeed.

---

[62] www.Merriam-webster.com

Use your imagination to dream big and then build small by taking the initiative with the first step in executing your vision. Do your research, plan, ask for advice, and then go all out full speed ahead. It is all or nothing, no in between. Give it all you've got and have the mentality that you will succeed.

PRINCIPLES RECAP

1. Prayer alone cannot create the change you envision.
2. Without vision people live haphazardly.
3. Initiative is taking small steps or doing something even when you are in unknown territory.
4. The highest form of faith is preparation, planning and expectation.
5. Planning is more work than the actual work itself.
6. Take time to think and plan then initiate the steps in the plan.
7. You are responsible for planning, which controls time and change.
8. From your heart (mind) comes the ideas and creative process utilizing the gift of imagination.
9. You are responsible for the plan, God's responsibility is to guide you and provide access to the resources.
10. If your heart is right then your thoughts are right.
11. Your responsibility is to make sure you are planning according to your purpose.
12. Seek counsel on your ideas from a trusted Godly expert, mentor or spouse.
13. Plans are not a prison they can take detours.
14. To operate effectively in the Kingdom it requires 100% trust and faith.
15. Your old ways of thinking will not function in the Kingdom.
16. You are required to obey the laws, but must break the rules that society has engrained in you.
17. It is about everyone God wants to reach through you – it's not about you.
18. God is looking for dedicated, focused individuals with the right mentality.
19. An opportunity is right if it lines up with your vision.

Chapter 8

SAFEST PLACE ON EARTH

Life Lesson #6

"Everything in life submits to something in order to function, grow and prosper." - Dr. Myles Munroe

If you take a look at nature you will notice that everything submits to something in order to function, grow, and prosper. Plants must submit to the soil in order to have life. Fish must stay submitted to the water to stay alive. If they decided to come out of their environment, they will naturally die. Nobody has to kill them. That is a law of nature. The absence of authority brings self-destruction. Nature knows it place. However, I have found that many people rebel to the thought of being submitted to someone to their own detriment. They are not aware of their safe place. Regardless of how successful we might be or our position of power, we can never get to the place where we are not properly submitted to someone.

The *two safest places on earth are under authority and in a community.* However, we live in a rebellious generation with many people foregoing this important position of submission to authority. It is so important that God made sure you had both principles in place when you were born. Your parents are your authority and it is impossible to conceive without a community. A community starts with two people. Therefore you can see God's best intentions because you were already in place upon birth. His plan was for our childhood years to be under the authority of our parents, for our own advantage. Children are not automatically aware of the dangers and pitfalls of life. They must be trained and taught properly. Therefore, God's original intention is for every child to benefit from the principle of submitting to authority and thriving in a community of a family unit.

Authority is the safest place for all created things. When you discover this you will have true freedom; it also eliminates stress. We have seen authority abused and thus many have automatically rebelled from this vital principle. The key is to find Godly authority and submit to them.

The three most important decisions of my life are very clear to me.

1. The day I became a Kingdom citizen at age five.

2. The day I decided to marry Matthew.

3. The day I decided to become a mentee of Dr. Myles Munroe.

These three important decisions changed the course of my life forever in the best possible way.

David understood and honored his authority, even when King Saul was trying to murder him. Even when a Godly authority can be misguided, the principle still remains. If you are faithful to the principle, then God will honor your obedience and the outcome will be in your favor; it is guaranteed. Although it might appear to be contradictory in the flesh, just give it time.

Principles are powerful forces that guarantee a certain outcome as long as you remain faithful to them. That requires no gossip or slander; just being patient and obedient. David did not have to fight or overthrow King Saul for his rightful position of King. He allowed

God to deliver him in the proper timing. Do not sabotage the season you are in by taking matters in your own hands by force. It takes maturity and 100% trust in God to wait for the proper outcome and the season to come to an end. God honored David for his obedience to this principle.

Even the seemingly un-Godly people in your life who are in authority over you can still be used to direct your life, promote you, and bring favor and blessings. God has used my father unknowingly to lead and direct me throughout my lifetime. My job is to honor him. This is one of the Ten Commandments.

Jesus never claimed to do anything on His own. He was always referring to one of His authorities, God the Father. Sometimes we think we are not legitimate unless we use our own words. You should be quoting and referring to your authority. There is nothing subservient about this. You are giving credit where it is due.

I recall when Jesus' authority was questioned by the religious people of the day.

"By what authority are you doing these things?" they asked. "And who gave you this authority?"[63]

They did not ask where He got His power from, but rather who gave Him this authority. His response was interesting.

"Jesus replied, 'I will also ask you one question. If you answer me, I will tell you by what authority I am doing these things. John's baptism—where did it come from? Was it from heaven, or of human origin?'"[64]

He was telling them it came from John the Baptist, but He knew they questioned John's authority. They discussed it among

---

[63] Matthew 21:23
[64] Matthew 21:24-25a

themselves and said,

> "If we say, 'From heaven,' he will ask, 'Then why didn't you believe him?' But if we say, 'Of human origin'—we are afraid of the people, for they all hold that John was a prophet." So they answered Jesus, "We don't know." Then he said, "Neither will I tell you by what authority I am doing these things.[65]

Jesus Himself was a man under authority by another man, John the Baptist. You may wonder when did this happen. Wasn't Jesus under only the authority of God? Let's take a look at what Jesus did right before he started His ministry as an adult.

> "Then Jesus came from Galilee to the Jordan to be baptized by John."[66]

Before Jesus started any miracles or teaching His first act was to go and find John to be baptized. Baptism is simply the act of submitting to a school of thought. Plato and Aristotle baptized people and had disciples according to their school of thought. What was John the Baptists' school of thought? He had one message. "Repent, for the kingdom of heaven has come near."[67]

Therefore Jesus was baptized under the same school of thought. You come under the authority and school of thought of the one doing the baptizing. Religion has made it entirely different. The Kingdom of heaven has arrived. Let's see what Jesus' first statement was after the testing in the desert.

> "From that time on Jesus began to preach, 'Repent, for the kingdom of heaven has come near.'"[68]

---

[65] Matthew 21:25b-27
[66] Matthew 3:13
[67] Matthew 3:2
[68] Matthew 4:17

They had the same school of thought, or message. However, when John tried to deter him by proclaiming he was not worthy to baptize Jesus we must look closely at Jesus' response.

> "Jesus replied, "Let it be so now; it is proper for us to do this to fulfill all righteousness." Then John consented."[69]

Jesus said he must be baptized by John in order to be in right-standing. This means right positioning with authority. He had to activate this principle on the earth. This is the ultimate act of submission. Jesus traveled seventy miles by foot to find John. That took two and a half days. Sometimes we must look far and wide, but it is worth the search. We must not be hasty to start our ministry or life vision without setting this principle in place first. People confuse the anointing for their right to be heard or launch their ministry. Submission to authority gives you a right to be heard. Otherwise you are operating illegitimately. Sure you have the power, but do you have the authority?

Here's the Son of God, in the flesh abiding by the principles set by God. He himself had to submit to a man on the earth in order to be in right standing with God. Jesus could not exercise His power without being under proper authority. Some people get confused with power and titles, rather than the true issue being the principle of authority. I cannot stress to you enough the importance of a proper covering. If Jesus needed it, how evident is it that we do too.

Who are we to think we are exempt from submitting to authority? Where did we get this rebellious spirit from? Who do we think we are? Be wary of those who say they are only accountable or submitted to God. That is a dangerous and slippery slope. Jesus himself was submitted to a man. Never submit to anyone who is not submitted to someone. Papa Myles was submitted to five other men.

---

[69] Matthew 3:15

At any time they could go through his computer, his phone and even talk to his wife. He was fully submitted and under authority.

When Papa Myles passed away I spent time in prayer and fasting before I decided who I would submit and come under authority. I understand how important it is for my life, the vision, and the community of leaders I mentor. Yes, I am also under the authority of my husband. However, I still need someone with the proper perspective and who has the same school of thought; someone outside of my marriage who can speak into it. This man is known as a maestro and traveled with Papa Myles the last three years of his ministry. He was trained by the best and has the same school of thought. Do not limit yourself to someone in a pulpit, your authority may be found in the business field, sports arena or any other system.

Two things qualify someone in my mind to be my authority: a person of character and the same school of thought. Look for someone with these two qualities. Ask God, for it's vital to your life. Here are the benefits of submitting to authority found in Matthew 3:16.

> "As soon as Jesus was baptized, he went up out of the water. At that moment heaven was opened, and he saw the Spirit of God descending like a dove and alighting on him. And a voice from heaven said, 'This is my Son, whom I love; with him I am well pleased.'"

All of heaven opens for the submitted person. There is an anointing that comes with submission. God promotes you Himself. You do not have to toil, connive or push doors open for yourself. There is no need for self-promotion. It takes maturity to wait for God to open the doors for you. When He does, trust me, it is well worth the wait. You will experience a far better platform than you would have by manipulating one for yourself. I have seen this happen numerous times in my life.

In 2008 someone heard me teach the message of the Kingdom and offered to sponsor my TV airtime for an entire year. I had to pay for the production of the spots, but the airtime was taken care of. It was not my idea to be on TV, but clearly it was God wanting to promote His message. I realize fully that it is not about me but His message and agenda.

Recently it happened again, someone else said this message needs to be on TV for more people to hear and they would sponsor everything; production and airtime, which costs around $20,000.

One of the most humbling times was when Papa Myles invited me to speak at his Kingdom Training Seminar in 2012 and every year since. I was a diligent student attending the seminar every year taking copious notes since 2009. Now three years later he invited me to be a teacher. What an honor to teach in my mentors' pulpit. I do not take that privilege lightly. He gave me a platform and I never once promoted myself. He said he had heard me teach on a video he saw that I had posted on Facebook. I never emailed him a video or told him I am an anointed woman of God. I just sat year after year learning and diligently applying the principles to my life. Every time he spoke in Florida, I was there. I would sit anywhere in the audience, sometimes undetected just to learn. I did not need to be in his face or sit on the front row. I just needed to be in the right atmosphere to learn. I was not pursuing him, but rather this knowledge of the truth.

Another instance was a phone call I received at work in 2013. It was a well-known business, inspirational speaker whom I had never met, but was aware of who he was. He had spoken at many of Dr. Myles Munroe's leadership summits. He was in Orlando and inquired about influential business people to a friend of mine. My friend recommended for him to call and meet me. Next thing I know, he stopped by the hotel for the afternoon and I showed him the area and we had dinner with my husband. Then I began speaking on a panel at his conference in the fall. The next year in 2014 he invited me to be a 'power speaker' along with my mentor, Dr. Myles Munroe! Are you kidding me? What a privilege to share the same platform with my mentor! I still am amazed. Later, I learned that he had asked Dr. Munroe his recommendation for me to be a power speaker, and Dr. Munroe said he gave his utmost blessing. You see what God did? I had nothing to do with it. My mentor promoted me.

> "When you are under the ultimate authority, you are protected so that you can complete the purpose of your personal authority."
> -Dr. Myles Munroe

That is the power of submission to authority. Again, I must reiterate, God is not a respecter of persons. Whatever area of influence you are gifted in, God will promote you in public if you are diligent in private and properly under authority. Just like he did with David to give him the throne of Israel. He was tested and passed the test. You must trust the process and pass the test.

Now here's the catch. There is a time for everyone to be tested. This is the fourth thing that happened to Jesus after He was baptized. He was led immediately by the Holy Spirit to be tempted in the desert. You are not qualified or prepared to face the devil until you have been properly submitted. This is a pitfall for many. They have no covering for protection. Once Jesus was under authority, He was qualified and covered to face the enemy and pass the tests. Then Jesus left the desert FULL of the Holy Spirit and thus His ministry started. He was legal.

Makes me wonder how many headless, illegal people are running around representing God without any protection. That is very dangerous ground. **Never trust anyone who has power but no authority.**

Let us recap the four results of submitting to authority:

1. Heaven opens.

2. God spoke to the crowd. He will promote you.

3. The anointing of the Holy Spirit is upon you.

4. You will be tested and qualified for the assignment on your life if you pass the tests.

There was a time Jesus was utterly amazed by a Roman centurion, a commander in the Roman army. He approached Jesus one day and asked Him to heal his servant who was paralyzed and suffering terribly. Jesus offered to go to his house to heal the man. The commander's response shocked Jesus.

"The centurion replied, 'Lord, I do not deserve to have you come under my roof. But just say the word, and my servant will be healed. For me I am a man under authority, with soldiers under me. I tell this one, 'Go,' and he goes; and that one, 'Come,' and he come. I say to my servant, 'Do this,' and he does it.'"[70]

The Bible states that this amazed Jesus and he responded:

"Truly I tell you, I have not found anyone in Israel with such great faith."[71]

This kind of faith Jesus had not seen anywhere. The Roman commander had been watching Jesus and understood the principle of authority. He was a man under authority. The key to Jesus' life was not power, but the authority to take away sin and heal people.[72]

Jesus told the Roman commander:

---

[70] Matthew 8:8-9
[71] Matthew 8:10b
[72] Matthew 9:6a

"Go! Let it be done just as you believed it would." And his servant was healed at that moment."[73]

Now let's take a look at how authority is received.

"Jesus called his twelve disciples to him and gave them authority to drive out impure spirits and to heal every disease and sickness."[74]

Jesus gave his twelve disciples authority. Therefore, authority is delegated and therefore can be recalled. It is a privilege and borrowed. If for some reason someone violates the trust of the people by a lack of character, they must step down and take time to be restored. The season of restoration is determined by the authority.

Now let's talk about your personal authority. Your authority is found in your legal area of domain established by God according to your gifting and life assignment. This is where you shine; I call it the sweet spot in life. You have the power to operate in your gifting, but true authority gives it a legal right to activate the power. In other words, your authority is only legal when you are under legal authority. Authority needs authority to be released properly. Otherwise your gift can destroy you. It can sabotage your entire life without having proper accountability. You can only go so far in this state. If you want to excel, then go low. Be humble and submit yourself to someone else. This is the only way to go up.

What does proper authority look like? Here are a few traits.

- They want nothing from you, nor can they benefit from you.
- They do not expect anything from you.
- They never manipulate abuse or misguide you.
- They genuinely desire for you to exceed them someday.

---

[73] Matthew 8:13
[74] Matthew 10:1

I will never forget one summer day in Peru of July 2014. I was sitting in the green room of a large amphitheater with Dr. Myles Munroe, his wife Ruth, and the Spanish translator from California. The translator was a pastor who asked if I was a speaker. Papa Myles spoke up and said "Oh yes, she is wonderful. I have her speak at my conferences. Trista is wise and she will be greater than me. One day it will all come together."

Here I sat with the greatest communicator and man of God of our time and he's saying I will be greater than him! Who does that? Only a confident true mentor of God can say it and believe it. He was stating another principle of submission: Whomever you submit to, you become greater than. If you see people who are great, do not compete with them, just submit to them. I saw a lot of people trying to compete with Papa Myles, which is counter-productive. A wise person will just submit to a great person.

Most importantly the true mark of a mentor is they make themselves unnecessary. They don't keep you dependent on them, although they are available for you when needed. Only an insecure mentor will keep you dependent for their own security. They have a need to be needed. Jesus said to his disciples, "How long must I be with you? How long shall I put up with you?"[75] There comes a time when the mentor expects you to be proactive and apply what you have learned. A baby does not remain at the mother's milk stage for ever. It is for a season, so stay submitted.

Jesus addressed leaders exercising illegitimate authority over others and stated that it would not be so with his disciples. Then he gave them the formula for greatness. By serving one another with your gift and He demonstrated with His life what that looked like.

---

[75] Matthew 17:17

"Jesus called them together and said, "You know that those who are regarded as rulers of the Gentiles lord it over them, and their high officials exercise authority over them. Not so with you. Instead, whoever wants to become great among you must be your servant, and whoever wants to be first must be slave of all. For even the Son of Man did not come to be served, but to serve, and to give his life as a ransom for many."[76]

It would be remiss of me to fail to mention the one other safe place on earth. It is found in a community. You were born into a community and for your protection remain in one throughout your lifetime. A community is simply a group of like-minded individuals who hold the same set of values and belief system. In the Kingdom of God a community also submits to a spiritual authority and is unified by a corporate responsibility and accountability. What separates one community from another is one word: *culture*. Your lifestyle, attitude and belief system separates you from other communities.

Isolation is the most dangerous place for an individual. God did not create people to succeed alone. Your family is the first community God intended for one to experience. As you mature and find your way in life, be mindful to seek out a community of people who you identify with. Many people find this in a church, some in a certain group of friends, others in a hobby or sport.

When I left religion I formed my own community in 2009 by starting a Bible study for ladies in my home. Then it grew into a beautiful, diverse community of like-minded leaders. We have various backgrounds and ethnic roots but the one thing we have in common is a Kingdom mentality. There is nothing more beautiful in my eyes than this. I love the richness found in a community with a diversity of backgrounds, yet the same mindset.

---

[76] Mark 10:42-45

A community looks out for one another's needs, supports each other, and inherits the vision for God's purpose in their region. The role of a community is to protect, preserve and develop the individual. You are a product of a community and become just like the community you are part of. In my community when someone has a need, such as rent we all chip in together and help provide for this need. However, this is only after they have given something to someone. They have been trained to activate the principle of giving first, and then we come together and support them.

The wrong community can contaminate an individual. We see this happening with gangs and terrorist groups, to name a few. We see people joining a desired community at college, sororities and fraternities. Peer pressure is nothing but community pressure. Being part of the wrong community can destroy and sabotage your future. Choosing the right community is detrimental to your future and the future generations.

> "If you want to go fast, go alone. If you want to go far, go together."
> -African proverb

In a community everything you do affects others. People cannot separate their private life from their public life. They must be one in the same. Accountability and transparency are necessary for you to flourish and mature.

So what happened when one person was disobedient in the nation of Israel? Joshua could not understand why they were losing battles to their enemies. God told him because there was sin in the camp. One man's misbehavior was causing the entire nation to suffer. They found Achan who had taken some spoils from the enemy and hid them in the ground in his tent. Joshua confronted him and asked, "Why have you brought this trouble on us?"[77] Then they

---

[77] Joshua 7:25

stoned the entire family and burned everything they owned. I know that sounds extreme, but this was the consequence of their disobedience.

A community is more important than the individual. The community must be protected at all cost. Anything that can bring destruction or division within a community must be dealt with promptly. God's original passion was to establish a Kingdom community on the earth that reflects the Kingdom culture of heaven. A group of people, a community who have His culture. That's the bottom line. When Isaac blessed Jacob he said:

> "May God Almighty bless you and make you fruitful and increase your numbers until you become a community of peoples."[78]

Jesus prayed for Kingdom culture to come to the earth. It is found in people, a community of like-minded people on earth, just like it is in Heaven. Religion works against God's program, by teaching to escape and be raptured to heaven. Jesus wants us to influence the earth through community with the culture of heaven; a group of people with morals, ethics and values, to reflect forgiveness and obedience to God. He did not say He wanted individual saints. We have been taught that our faith is private and we separate it from our public responsibility. It is one in the same. It's the core of who we are. The attraction of this Heavenly culture should be so strong until it should be the dominant culture on earth. Our behavior should be day and night compared to the other communities. This is the will of God for the earth. It was His desire for Israel to represent Him on the earth, as an example to the other nations. I believe that is why He was so adamant for them to not marry outsiders; they worshipped false gods. Then the women would train the children to worship other gods and the culture would be contaminated. This is why we

---

[78] Genesis 28:3

are told to be equally yoked with our spouse. You are creating a family community and it is vital that the values and belief systems are the same.

To recap, the two most important places to be in life are found in a healthy community and under authority. This ultimately brings protection to your life, your future, and even future generations. These are vital components to success in your life. Whatever you do make sure you are found in the safest places on earth.

PRINCIPLES RECAP

1. The absence of authority brings self-destruction.
2. Find Godly authority and submit to them.
3. God will even use ungodly people in authority over you to direct your life, promote you, and bring favor and blessings.
4. All of heaven opens for a submitted person.
5. God will promote you in public if you are diligent in private and submitted to proper authority.
6. Trust the process and always be sure to pass the test.
7. Never trust anyone who has power, but no authority.
8. Your authority is found in your sphere of influence.
9. You have the power to operate in your gifting, but true authority gives it a legal right to activate the power.
10. Your authority is only legal when you are under legal authority.
11. Whoever you submit to you become greater than.
12. Under authority and in a community are the safest places to be.

Chapter 9

WHO IS YOUR SOURCE?

Life Lesson #7

"True wealth is having access to what you need when you need it."
-Dr. Myles Munroe

People around the world are chasing after the mighty dollar. This problem is quite prevalent in our culture, regardless of our religious affiliations. People risk their lives, negate their family, murder, steal, manipulate and lie for it. Yet it still seems to elude them eventually one way or another. How did we get to this place of referring to ourselves as rats, in an endless, self-defeating or pointless pursuit?[79] Just working to live and living to work. We have been conditioned to think that we are our own source. If your ideas are wrong, then your life will be wrong. This constant demand causes stress and anxiety that your body was not created to handle. We know there has to be more to life than paying bills and dying. I understand why so many people turn to alcohol, and illegal and prescription drugs to cope. This lifestyle started in Genesis chapter 3 after the rebellion of Adam and Eve. God told Adam because of his disobedience, "Cursed is the ground because of you; through painful toil you will eat food from it

---

[79] www.en.wikipedia.org

all the days of your life."[80] This is the first place you find the word *toil* in the scriptures. The definition of toiling is *"exhausting labor or effort; to move slowly and with difficulty[81]; long strenuous fatiguing labor.[82]"*

There was no toiling in the Garden of Eden, God only told Adam to work and take care of it[83]. In other words, manage it. Working is a joy when you are operating in your passion, your purpose. When you are doing what you love to do you don't want to stop to eat a meal or go to sleep. You can do it day and night. Your passion is your fuel because you are doing what you were born to do. However, most people are caught in the rat race of life. Who has time for that? It is a curse. Jesus redeemed us back to the original plan of God. Found in Genesis chapters 1 and 2 are the original will and intent of God for mankind on the earth. The curse happened in Genesis chapter 3 and the remainder of the Bible is a repair program to get us back to the first two chapters of Genesis where it all started in the Garden of Eden. Here's where I want to point out something fascinating. The word Eden is a Hebrew word that is expressed with five strokes in meaning.

- Spot
- Moment
- Presence
- Open Door
- Delightful Place

The Garden of Eden has never been located because it's an environment. It is a word used to define the spot of an open door of

[80] Genesis 3:17b
[81] www.TheFreeDistionary.com
[82] www.Merriam-webster.com
[83] Genesis 2:15

the pleasant presence of God. Eden is a spot where there is an open access to heaven. This is where you were created to function. Outside of this environment, God said Adam would surely die. We cannot function as intended outside of the presence of God. He is our source. Animals and plants were created out of the ground. If you pull a plant out of the ground it automatically dies, because it has been removed from its source. Animals eat the plants and other animals, because they come from the same source, as does our flesh. Our spirits are the same material as God, so we need the same environment as His. You do not have a spirit, you are a spirit. He showed us how the original Adam operated by having dominion over the fish, sickness, and finances. This is what He redeemed us back to. Unfortunately, many are living so far below our original state designed and redeemed for us. This is the ultimate reason why I wrote this book.

Let us look at God's function. His personal name is actually YHWH meaning, "I AM". In English we add vowels to make it "YAHWEH". One of the ways YHWH has been translated is "The Self-Existent One." So we see by this that God self-exists all by Himself, without any dependencies whatsoever. Everything else in the universe depends on something. Your lungs need oxygen; trees produce oxygen and need soil, sun and water to survive. Oxygen is molecules; molecules need molecular cohesion, etc…. I think you see the pattern. Everything in the universe is derived and dependent on a source, except God Himself. If you recall Jesus referred to God as Abba. This is an intimate term for God as Father. It is a term expressing warm affection and a dependent relationship with a father. This is also the role of the Holy Spirit to lead you to a relationship with God where you recognize Him as your Father and call Him such. Now what does the word Father mean? It means both *source and sustainer.* God your Father is both a source and sustainer to those that consider themselves His children. His job is to be your source and to sustain you throughout your lifetime and into eternity.

How comforting I find this to be. It takes all the pressure off of me for trying to be my own source. My concern is to have the faith of a child that says Father God has everything taken care of. Therefore my main focus is on obeying Him, which causes me to be in right standing. One of the benefits of right standing is having ACCESS to heaven's resources; the open door to my SOURCE, God the Father. I am aware that He is my source and sustainer. However, to their own detriment, too many people confuse themselves and other people as their source. They may think their job is their source, their boss, maybe a rich relative or a sugar daddy. Many consider these as their source. However, Father God is our source and He uses various resources to provide for us. We will continue to toil in life until we fully comprehend this principle.

In February 2014, I sat in a retreat in Naples, Florida, for the executive trustees of Dr. Myles Munroe's leadership organization, ITWLA. Dr. Munroe explained these different types of resources:

1. People
2. Experience
3. Time
4. Relationships
5. Energy
6. Monetary

Then He talked about the Ultimate Source, God the Father. This gives us the capacity to tap into something beyond the earth, which makes us unlimited with Divine ideas. He said there will be moments that we will know how to fix things (like Moses at the Red Sea). DONT FORGET THE GOD FACTOR!!!

So that we are clear:

God the Father = Ultimate Source

People, money, relationships, time, experience & energy = Resources

Now here's where I clarify how different the economy system of the nations and the Kingdom of God work. The problem is that many of us live in a democracy, which promotes ownership. This spirit of ownership creates many problems. It creates frustration, depression, lack, theft, scarcity, stress, and has limitations. We take pride in ownership and this causes huge problems. Our cultures thrive on ownership. America was built on this concept and has become a mental stronghold. Ownership is a curse. Once you own something it is your responsibility to maintain it and fix it. I think of a popular hip-hop song from the 90's *"Mo money, mo problems."* The more things we accumulate, the more money it takes to maintain them. God hates hoarding, for this only builds up a dam and blocks the flow of our resources.

The Kingdom of God functions different in the form of a commonwealth system. God's economy has nothing to do with money; which is the source of worry. The currency in His economy system is Faith. This is how we operate in His country. In a commonwealth the King is obligated to oversee the welfare of His citizens. There is always a bountiful supply of resources for the citizens to access. There is equal access by all the citizens to the provisions and protection of the government of a Kingdom. The most important principle of a Kingdom is Lordship. You see how different this is from a democracy; this concept does not even exist in it. As I am writing this Greece is facing bankruptcy as a nation. This is the birthplace of democracy. We think this is the best form of government that man came designed. But it does not compare to the government of God; a government from another world, that operates in the world I live in. The earth was never designed to function independently of heaven. We need constant access.

Let's take a look at God's solution for ownership. What did the people of Jesus' time refer to Him as? LORD. What does Lord mean? It means ADONI or owner. Jesus is Lord. He is the owner. He also called himself a King. The King owns everything. This is how kingdoms operate as a commonwealth. The citizens do not own anything, but they have access to everything. He told Adam in Genesis 2.

"And the Lord God commanded the man, "You are free to eat from any tree in the garden;"[84]

Adam was given access not ownership. In essence Adam was free to partake of the food in God's garden (except the tree of knowledge of good and evil). When you take ownership of things you stop access and the government shuts down on you.

If you can grasp this concept of a kingdom then you will start living. Rather than chasing resources, they will be attracted to you. I see this in my life all the time. Your priorities in life are to chase after the Kingdom and remain in right standing. Purse your life vision in order to bear fruit and watch the resources that the King owns chasing after you. This is no pipe dream; it's a reality. This is why I'm so passionate about this principle, it works. I refuse to toil in life. I am always working diligently on my life assignment and God's responsibility is to provide for it. He is obligated to me as a citizen in right-standing to be my source. That's not what He does, it's WHO HE IS! It's His nature.

"He is not obligated to pay for the bills you create, but to pay for the bills He created you to create." -Dr. Myles Munroe

I walk in the understanding that God owns everything on the earth and He can distribute them however He pleases. He owns the banks, all the buildings, all the vehicles, everything! Need proof? Alright.

"The earth is the LORD's, and everything in it, the world, and all who live in it"[85]

---

[84] Genesis 2:16

Wealth in the Kingdom is: **having access to what you need when you need it**. That is true wealth. Our idea of wealth is having what we need before we need it. This is a stockpile mentality. However, God owns everything and can distribute it to you when it is needed. I pray you can truly grasp this vital concept to Kingdom living. Otherwise, you will live a very stressful life relying on yourself as your own source. God is your source and He uses His resources so you can accomplish what He created you to do on the earth.

I also understand He can turn the heart of anyone, anywhere to give you favor. I experience this more often than not. It truly is exciting to live this way. I think God gets so much joy in surprising us like little children at Christmas time. He's just looking for those who have the kind of faith that is required. Like Jesus said, "when the Son of Man comes, will he find faith on the earth?"[86]

"No one has ever become poor from giving."
- Maya Angelou

It is your job to activate this principle within the economy system of His Kingdom. You must prove you do not own anything by giving. You do not give to receive, you give to obey and prove you do not own anything. However our culture tells us differently, *"Get as much as you can, as fast as you can and keep it!"* What a selfish mentality we live by. GET GET GET! In the Kingdom its opposite is: GIVE GIVE GIVE!

His Kingdom operates by giving. Giving activates the economy and forces people (resources) to be multiplied back to you. That is a much better system then we have in democracy! Giving keeps the flow of resources constantly moving and recycling to others. Then

---

[85] Psalm 24:1
[86] Luke 18:8b

God can trust you with resources, for you realize you are a conduit. So when God gives you something it may be for the season that it is needed. When He tells you to pass it along to someone else, you have no issue, for you know you were a steward of it all along. That is why I had no issues giving cars away. They were not junk either. Since that time, I have been surprised by three lovely vehicles. My standards weren't ever brand names, but the function of them. I like sporty SUV's because I can transport items for the hotel and when I had my baby I had more room and felt more protected. So the purpose of a thing is more my interest, not the image or brand of the car, but if it functions according to my needs.

If God gives you something and you do not use it for its intended purpose, He can recall it. As Dr. Myles Munroe taught us: "When purpose is not known abuse is inevitable." If you are not sure about the purpose of a resource then ask God. When we acquired a jet recently I had a conversation with Matthew to be sure we were well aware of the purpose of it. It was important for both of us to have the same mindset, for if we only used it for golf trips and pleasures, then I know we

> "He is not obligated to pay for the bills you create, but to pay for the bills He created you to create."
> -Dr. Myles Munroe

would eventually lose it. I have access to it whenever I need it for my life vision. I'm doing God's business and Matthew is financing it through his business gift. I never received the bill for fuel when I took my team of leaders to Haiti. I do not have to raise the money for maintaining it and staffing it with two pilots. I do not want to own a plane on paper; I realize that all I need is access to one. I just jump on it when God sends me on assignment. I don't have the stress of insuring it, maintaining it or filling it with fuel. It is the most beautiful set up in the world! Trust me; access is more important than ownership.

I have made it a life-long habit since I was five years old to tithe and give offerings. Tithing is simply the Kingdom's taxation system. You pay 10% taxes on what you make. Take note that tithing does not prosper you, it simply positions you properly. You can only give offerings after you have paid your taxes (tithe) to the storehouse, where you are being fed spiritually. The Bible states that you are a thief if you keep the taxes that belong to God, therefore He will send the devourer. I think of it as the IRS in our country. They come after you and put you in jail. When you are in jail you are no longer a citizen of the USA and have no rights. You become an illegal citizen if you don't pay your taxes. I have the right to demand my rights as a citizen in the Kingdom of God as long as I am a good-standing citizen with the government. Let's take a look at what Malachi says:

> "Will a man rob God? Yet you have robbed me! But you say, 'In what way have we robbed You?' 'In tithes and offerings. You are cursed with a curse, For you have robbed Me, even this whole nation. Bring all the tithes into the storehouse,

> That there may be food in My house, And try Me now in this," Says the Lord of hosts, "If I will not open for you the windows of heaven and pour out for you such blessing that there will not be room enough to receive it."[87]

Windows in Hebrew is an idiom for *access*. He will give you access to unseen resources if you pay your taxes (tithes). You do not need prayer to open windows, you need principles. Pay your taxes AND be a giver. This activates the economy system of the government of God. He recommends you to test Him by this principle, 'Try Me

---

[87] Malachi 3:8-10

now in this'. He's daring you to activate it! In essence He's saying, *Go ahead give it a try and see if I won't respond.*

I will never forget it was Super Bowl Sunday 1986 with the Bears playing against the New England Patriots. The Bears were quite popular that year. That morning at church, during offering time I recalled I only had 67 cents to my name. As a twelve year old, I felt so bad that was all I could give to God. I did not even have a $1 bill to give. So I gave what I had and went about my business. That evening I attended the Super Bowl party with my family at one of their friend's house. They were holding a little raffle potluck game for $1 a ticket. One of dad's friends was nice enough to offer me a few tickets. You know this is very exciting for a child. Guess who won the raffle lottery? ME! Guess how much it was? $67.00 exactly. That was my hundred-fold return. I told my dad my amazing testimony and boy did I learn an unforgettable principle that day. So as long as I can remember I have always given my taxes to God.

One year while living in the trailer park, my parents went away for the weekend. I was either nine or ten years old. I stayed with an older lady, Mary Parmagianni across the street. She used to give me circus peanut candy. Dad gave me $20 for the weekend in case we went out to eat or I needed something. Well as it turns out, Mary was on a lot of medicine and always complaining about her stack of bills on her table and how she lived on a budget. All I remember was I felt so badly because she was in pain, I believe it was arthritis and she did not have much money. When it was time for me to go back home, I left the $20 bill under her placemat for her to find when she wiped down her table each night. A few days later my dad and mom approached me and asked if I gave Mary the money they had given me. I said yes, she needs it. My dad opened his wallet and gave me a $100 bill! I then corrected his math by mentioning that 100 fold of $20 is $200, so he gave me another $100 bill! What a lesson for a child. Again, I was amazed how easy this principle operates, every time. My faith has remained the same, and I understand the principles. I'm telling you there is something about having child-like faith. It is a tough road without it.

Just one more story. Jesus told a parable that most of us missed. The story of the Prodigal Son found in Luke 15:11-32.

The story starts out with the younger son demanding his father to 'give me what is mine.' You can see the spirit of ownership operating here. He then went on a trip to a foreign land and squandered everything indulging in his pleasures. Then recession hit the country he was visiting and he had no money left to purchase food. So he found a job feeding the pigs. He began wishing he could have his belly filled with food just like the pigs. The pigs were better off than him.

Then Jesus said a very important statement, "When he came to his senses." You see, we must give people the freedom of free will and the time to hopefully come to their senses. The father never chased after his son. So the young man came to his senses and says, 'Even my father's servants have food to eat and I am sitting here starving. I will go back to my father ask for forgiveness and ask to work as a servant.' The father welcomes him back with open arms and throws a big party. But Jesus did not stop there. He continued the parable with the older son who became angry and resented the fact that he was the obedient son who worked hard for his father all these years and never squandered his resources. His dad looked at him and said, "My son, you are always with me, and **everything I have is yours.**"[88] There it is! You see his oldest, obedient son had accesses to everything he ever wanted at anytime he needed it.

> "Access is more important than ownership."
> - Dr Myles Munroe

---

[88] Luke 15:31

Jesus always focused on righteousness, rather than the sin of the prodigal son. The oldest son had access to whatever he needed because his father owned everything. I pray that you will never worry or toil another day in your life. Worry is not a concept or vocabulary word found in the Kingdom. Jesus told us not to worry about anything in our life.[89] You only worry if you think you are your own source, and then you will find yourself toiling. My friend, life is too short for this.

[89] Matthew 6:25

PRINCIPLES RECAP

1. Everything in the universe is derived and dependent on a source, except God himself.
2. Access to heaven's resources is one of the benefits of being in right standing.
3. Don't forget the God factor.
4. We own nothing, but have access to everything.
5. Wealth in the Kingdom is having access to what you need when you need it.
6. God, who is your source, provides you His resources so you can accomplish what He created you to do on the earth.
7. You do not give to receive, you give to obey and prove you do not own anything.
8. Giving activates the Kingdom economy and forces resources to be multiplied back to you.
9. God can trust you with resources, if you realize you are a conduit.
10. Access is more important than ownership.
11. Tithing is the Kingdom's taxation system and positions you properly.
12. You can only give after you have paid your taxes to the storehouse where you are being mentally and spiritually fed.
13. You can make demands to the Kingdom as long as you are a citizen in good standing with the government.
14. You do not need prayer to open windows, you need principles.
15. We must give people the freedom of free will and the time to hopefully come to their senses.
16. Worrying ties Gods hands and causes you to toil

CONCLUSION

Jesus came to earth and explained the Kingdom of God and to give us the keys (principles) to live an abundant life. In this book I have documented seven of the most important key factors that have fashioned my life, as well as many more. No matter what stage of life you find yourself in, if applied they will work for you too.

I pray this book has brought clarity and simplicity to the principles of God through my life stories. Likewise, you must also teach others what you have learned through your own testimonies of applying the principles of God to your life, business and community. I would love to hear from you.

APPENDIX

The Kingdom of God Ambassador's Pledge

"I confess Jesus Christ as my Lord, my Savior, my Redeemer,
and my King.
I accept the Holy Spirit, the Governor of Heaven, to live
in me now, forever.
I accept the word of God as my Constitution and the Laws of this
Constitution, and I pledge to obey them until I die.
I receive the mandate to go into all the world and take the gospel of
the kingdom of God into every nation, every system, and every
neighborhood.
I receive this solemn pledge, and I will not violate the laws of God.
I will obey my King without question.
Amen."

Because of your confession, I confer on you in the Name of the
Father, Son, and the Holy Spirit, the Ambassadorial credentials of the
kingdom of Heaven.
May He put upon your shoulders, His sword; and knight you as
Kings and Priests upon the earth.
May you walk boldly without fear.
May you never be afraid of the eyes of those who look at you, for
you are the great one.
He who is in you is greater than he who is in the world.
He who is in you is greater than He who is in the world.
He who is in you is greater than he who is in the world.
Therefore, go boldly and declare the kingdom of God.
And lo, I am with you always even unto the end of this age, and no
man shall stand before you.

Today, you are pledged to be God's Ambassadors.
Represent the Kingdom well and be afraid of nothing, for the LORD
is with you.
And if the LORD is with you, who can be against you?
Today, you have been transformed.

Figure It Out

Recommended Readings

- Gospels of Matthew, Mark, Luke and John seven times.

- *Rediscovering the Kingdom* – Dr. Myles Munroe

- *The Most Important Person on Earth* – Dr. Myles Munroe

- *The Principles and Power of Vision* – Dr. Myles Munroe

- *The Spirit of Leadership* – Dr. Myles Munroe

- *Re-discovering Faith* – Dr. Myles Munroe

- *Overcoming Crisis* – Dr. Myles Munroe

About The Author

Trista Sue Kragh, an alumni of Oral Roberts University, is president and founder of Kingdom Community International, a global leadership training and mentorship organization. She serves as a trustee of her mentor and spiritual father, the late Dr. Myles Munroe's leadership organization, ITWLA. She traveled with Dr. Munroe to many nations meeting with government officials.

In 2015, Trista Sue opened her own office with the focus to expand the mentorship and leadership training with the vision of "Changing the destiny of nations through leadership training." She operates the Bayfront Inn in Naples, Florida, utilizing her twenty years of hotel experience as an international business and leadership speaker. The practical principles she shares were proven to be very successful through the recession, and even in her involvement in launching her husband's architecture firm during the same period of economic decline. Due to their testimony, they are found in many 'closed' countries teaching time - tested business principles.

Matthew Kragh, her husband, is a competitive golfer and award-winning architect. They have a son, Maverick, and a baby on the way.

Resources From Trista Sue

"Inspiring individuals to discover and manifest their full potential through intentional training"

Resources and training opportunities available online and on
www.TristaSue.com.

E-learning courses/Mentorship for producing Agents of Change

Trista Sue Kragh

'Naples-Embassy' live streaming and video archives

Trista Sue – Entrepreneur (Public Profile Page)
Kingdom Community Int.

Webinars – broadcast biweekly

Retreats held annually at the Bayfront Inn Naples, Florida.

www.BayfrontInnNaples.com

Personal Email: **Trista@TristaSue.com**

Office Contact

Kingdom Community International
975 6th Ave South, Suite #200
Naples, Florida 34102 USA
Phone: (239) 465-0409
Executive Administrator: Debra Horner
E-mail: DHorner@tristasue.com

Made in the USA
Lexington, KY
27 July 2015